2020
Astrology
Forecast

Tim Stephens
www.astralreflections.com

Disclaimer:

The information in this book is intended only as an informative guide and nothing in this book may be considered personal advice. Tim Stephens in not a doctor, and none of the statements about health and wellbeing are medical advice; they do not substitute, and are not intended to conflict with or countermand a physician or health care provider's advice or medical care. Please consult your physician or other health care provider — without delay — if you are experiencing any symptoms or have any concerns pertaining to information contained in this book.

Photo and image credits: Unless otherwise noted, all photographs and images are copyright. Constellation: Image by Gerd Altmann from Pixabay

First Edition:
E-Book   published Dec. 31, 2019
Paperback   published Jan. 7, 2020
ISBN-13:   978-1-6546-3596-1
Publisher: 306608 B.C. Ltd., Canada
                Tim Stephens
                WWW.ASTRALREFLECTIONS.COM

Contents

Tim Stephens

Tim Stephens' syndicated horoscope column (now a blog) has been published for 39 years. His astrology blog is read world-wide and his clients come from North America and Europe, Russia, China, India, Australia, Malaysia, Mexico and South Africa.

Tim is a trusted, 90% accurate astrologer. He has made many stunningly correct predictions for decades, including:

- rise of the Dow from 800 in 1980 to 28,000 presently,
- interest rate fall from 12% to presently 1%,
- AIDS,
- Chernobyl,
- October/86 stock crash,
- space shuttle Challenger explosion,
- first Gulf War, • 2006-08 credit crash,
- metro-sexualism,
- FBI corruption, and more.

To learn more about Tim's work, visit www.astralreflections.com

Introduction

This book delivers Astrologer Tim Stephens' forecast of 2020's events and influences for all 12 signs.

Tim has studied the year ahead for every sign, Aries to Pisces, and put his insights and predictions for you — your personal 2020 opportunities and cautions — accompanied by specific dates and advice:

- Start nothing periods
- Luck / Karma
- Love
- Career / Business
- Home / Family
- Finances / Investments / Debt
- Health

2020 brings a new major luck cycle for every sign, and this, too, is laid out for every sign.

World Predictions: 2020

2020's a sober year in which many of the pressures of 2018/19 will "explode" into dramatic events and "manifestos." (E.g., the Impeachment of Trump is really a manifesto by vengeful Democrats.)

Around the world, hierarchy-transforming tensions continue, though they abate briefly this Spring.

Riots/revolt will continue (mostly in "I" nations — Iraq, Iran, etc.) to 2026. In 2021/22, rebellion will be strongly repressed, but also in 21/22, rebels will begin forming a deeper, stronger base.

July to early January 2021 will bring dramatic, direct, sometimes violent action. Police and soldiers feel empowered. A short but intense war might occur in these months.

The U.S. "uncivil war," now in its third year, is just one stage of a world-wide transformation in which both communism and democracy will be replaced by a new system of government. I've been beating this drum since the 1980's. This transformation is well underway in China, and is in its "birthing stage" in America. The American crisis of change will climax in 2022. This transformation will focus on 4 main areas: children/youth/education, patriotism/"us," foreign relations, and sex.

Europe:

Overall, Europe will begin to recover economically. This will bring a nascent but noticeable rise in mood and hope, and in turn a fresh flowering of the arts.

Canada:

Canada will suffer very little disruption. Despite an inverted yield curve (usually a harbinger of recession) Canada will flow along rather peacefully, as usual, with no big collapses or dents in its economy. Justin Trudeau will cease being gaffe-prone by May, but he's likely to make a big one before then.

Iran/Iraq:

Iran will become extremely militant and aggressive July to December — but toward others, or their own citizens? (Might bomb the U.S. or its embassies — not just its ships. Might invade Iraq in a big way.) DO NOT visit during these months. Iraq will continue its revolt/riots for 6 more years.

China:

The upheavals in China's population, which have been occurring since 2009, will begin to slow down. The most dramatic of these upheavals, the massive and ongoing riots in Hong Kong, will oddly do an oxymoron: they will both expand on the top line or showy side, and shrink on the deeper or more fundamental side. This says that China's struggles with its population will be somewhat reduced, especially in the spring of 2020, and 2021 forward. (Note this is in contrast to more worldwide rebellion, which I mention elsewhere.)

U.S.A.:

This nation's struggles lie at the hub of the world's wheel. The present political crisis will alter the structure of democracy around the world — even in "communist" China.

Who wins the U.S. federal election in November? I'll opine on that in my blog, astralreflections.com, later.... The election winner will be the target of an assassination attempt. Oddly, this possibility lessens if Trump is re-elected.

U.S. politics might grow more violent, certainly more dramatic, from July to January, 2021.

The present "uncivil war" (which I forecast 4 years ago) will peak in 2022 — 3 years away. In 2021, "revolt" will hold hands with civil war, bringing — what?

(In 2018 or 19, I had an "image" of the National Guard surrounding Congress…or the White House…not sure what this means, or even if it will eventually occur.)

I think I heard that the U.S. Supreme Court will address the many personal tax-related fishing assaults on Donald Trump in June. If so, if June, Trump will win.

Trump's popularity will rise markedly from April to August. His main enemy, Adam Schiff, will be incensed, raging, July to December.

This period, July to December, the U.S. might show violence to other nations. Any martial stuff will be "police action" — but this one's bigger than any Trump has effected to date. (The biggest war involving the U.S. will occur in 2027 — maybe '28.)

The F.I.S.A. court judges will come under scrutiny, and should be indicted. (Though criminal charges are unlikely, as the elites protect the elites.)

Minor Players:

A big change for Nancy Pelosi, leader of the Dems in Congress. A fall in popularity coincides with her push for more power, this Spring and all 2021/22. Yet she might win a "victory" in the last 8 months.

Adam Schiff, the deceitful instigator of the impeachment drive against Trump, will be "protected" through April, but then the consequences begin. Schiff will be consumed by rage — and ambition — from July into January 2021. This might be his downfall.

3

Chuck Schumer, who leads the Democrats in the Senate, will suffer a down trend from May onward (through 2021).

The Clinton's reputations have been destroyed by their pedophilia and treason. Hillary's big downfall comes 2022 to mid-2023. Bill might bop along, untouched legally, until 2026. But Bill will suffer public disdain in Spring 2020, and all through 2021/22. This will hurt him deeply, as he loves to be admired.

Economy:

This Spring (of 2020) "unpredictability" will affect socializing, banks and land values. This might cause a "jerk" in the economy/stock market, but absent this the North American economy will chug along without major crisis.

Projects launched this Winter, Summer or Autumn (anywhere in the world — even in your own life) will last and grow for at least three decades, especially in business and government zones.

Banks are pressured, 2018 to 2026, but also grow more ambitious. Watch your bank stocks carefully this Spring, and again December into 2022.

Other Things:

NGO's and humanitarian organizations will shrink in 2021-2024. We might see a hint of this in Spring 2020. When I predicted in the late 1980's that universities would become corrupt for two centuries, I also included lawyers because the law is, in astrology, the same as universities. Judges are lawyers, and already swim in the same corrupt stew. The F.I.S.A. judges were crooked or criminally negligent when they kissed the rotting FBI's robes. Universities will continue their prejudiced teachings — for 200 years.

Technology and the Far Future

In 2020 a temporary dimming of the technological light begins, and 2021/22 will slow the advance of high tech. But 2024-26 will bring a resurgence of tech. This resurgence will show more dramatically what is already ongoing, advances in light, optics, oceanography (as a blanket term) and space/astrophysics.

In medicine the emphasis has been on structure and bureaucracy since 2009 — this continues to 2025. (Note the "free medical" platforms of U.S. Presidential candidates.) With eyes, circulation, viral diseases and water supply, great advances have occurred since 2011, and will until 2025.

Technology is on a rapid rise, and will continue so for another 200 years, to 2229. That year will start another era in history, lasting to 4452. The present era, from 2439 BC to 2229 AD, brought us monotheism (belief in one God) mathematics (beyond mere counting) the modern (Phoenician) alphabet, and of course technology.

The 2229-4452 AD era, as I've written before, will bring either a) an "angel" as wide as the horizon, or whatever that might mean in symbolic terms, or b) contact with other beings, or c) we cross the ocean of space to other stars.

Whether we want to be or not, we're angels, everyone of us (all part of the same angel, actually) slowly crawling along the spiritual road to angel-hood.

We've made pretty good progress in the last few millennia, and will make even more for the next 2 centuries. Then, as stated above, in approximately 2229 to the 4,000's, we rush toward that goal in ways and with a speed that would amaze us today. Spirituality and technology will merge and become one.

It's not apparent yet, but real estate will become a problem centuries down the road. I think we will see communal "groups" of maybe 500 to 10,000, rather than big cities.

ARIES

March 21 – April 19

Start nothing significant or important:
February 16 to March 9
June 18 to July 12
October 13 to November 3.

GENERAL:

For ten years, Aries, your career zone has been a sober, serious place, filled with power struggles and unseen forces of change. You might have gained great power, or struggled against great odds, especially in the last year. You might have felt the touch of destiny, but seldom of good luck.

In 2020, at last, that changes — a year of great good luck faces you in the whole area of ambitions, career, worldly standing and prestige relations. You're going up, Aries! — But read your "Luck" and "Karma" sections before you leap, as the first 4 months need some thought.

You will grab your life this year and direct it where you want to go, as you seldom have before. From July through December, your own planet, Mars, rumbles through Aries, imbuing you with extra courage, determination, and effectiveness. You really are setting your course this year, perhaps for a few to come.

In 2020 you will mold your life — or even create a new life.

You'll burn with intensity. People will step out of your way! For best results, mix that intensity with a sprinkling of empathy, gentleness and humour. Be assertive, confident and yield to your impulses this year (but read "Career" below for timing). Work hard, because a celebration, a "happy, social rest" will come all 2021 — and the harder you work now, the bigger your 2021 celebration will be.

Success in love and partnerships will depend on your communications and willingness to travel, especially from April to August. If single, you'll attract someone strongly the last half of 2020.

Neptune remains in your sector of gov't, management, large companies and institutions, from 2011 to 2025. Your hunches and intuition will be accurate in dealing with management types, civil servants, etc. This is also a good (the best) period for seeking advisors, mentors and agents.

These 15 years are the best period of your life to develop a relationship with spirit — God, karma, whatever you want to call it. Meditation is one road; simply sitting on the back porch and pondering your life, is another. Your home life is blessed January through April.

LUCK:

"Luck" is always of two kinds: the normal, daily or monthly luck that Jupiter (optimism and great worldly luck) and Venus (sweet love, attractions, and mild but good luck). And "karma," the ongoing result of actions we took and patterns we started and wove in the past, that now is rewarding us, or wrapping us in the punishing, restricting web of our own actions/consequences.

Jupiter:

Your main, great good luck this year focuses almost entirely on your career, your worldly standing, prestige relations and status in the community. (January to December 20 — the last 11 days give you a social boost — or begin to make a career wish come true.)

8

Venus:

Your love luck this year is highest in early January, early February to early March, September, first two-thirds of November, and the last half of December.

Karma:

Until May 5 — but only to then — your "bad karma" lies in career (read "Career" below) and status, prestige, ambition zones. E.g., this is a terrible time to appear before a judge. Same period is a splendid time to focus on home, children, and security. From May 6 to year's end, you will face a smooth, mellow, green path in conversations, letters, texts and emails, calls, visits, short trips, daily facts, figures and news, errands, paperwork and "making contact."

During the same period, avoid lawsuits, lawyers, international affairs, far travel and voyages, cultural/religious belief systems, social rituals (e.g., a wedding) fame, publishing and most intellectual pursuits (e.g., higher education). These are doorways to eventual delay and disappointment, this May to early 2022.

If you want to improve your karma, pick up hitch-hikers, help little old ladies across the street, send a sweet, friendly note to lift someone's spirits, etc. In other words, be helpful in little, daily ways. Giving someone life advice, or propounding religious or other beliefs, will not help your karma. In fact, it might harm it.

Read/write a news article, NOT a book or long thesis. Pursue facts, not ideas.

LOVE:

Ah, love. First, the big picture: March begins three years (to March 2023) of a quieter or more sober, mature social life. In many cases, and on many occasions, your career and social spheres will intermingle. This is not a bad influence, only a maturing one — In 2021, you will likely begin/create a whole new, powerful social circle that can be in your life for decades.

For the first 5 months, romance is a bit changeable. January to mid-February sees you being chased, perhaps by an intelligent, outgoing, temperamental person.

He/she will be very social, or draw you into a group, but he/she also knows/senses some of your weaknesses or secrets, so be "aware."

Your physical charms shine in February. March will bring a sensual attraction, but it's "only physical" — true love and excitement are missing.

Your social life grows a lot livelier in April, as your charisma rises, but so does social activity. Woe to those who would exclude you from "the club" this month. You might meet someone instrumental to your future career success this April, and to some degree all year.

May is for sensual (but not really romantic) attractions. (However, from 2019 to 2026, sensual relationships will be very friendly and optimistic, and many Aries-Taurus marriages will take place — tho' I don't usually recommend these.)

During May and June, many communications take place, with your spouse, lover, or prospect. You, or he/she, or both, are wrestling with indecision. A former flame or "ex" might appear. The indecision will dissolve by late summer, so be patient.

(A former flame might re-appear in October, too, but this one was almost exclusively sexual, and might not have a big future.)

You will be extremely magnetic from July through December — but will you be charming, gentle and understanding also? Well…that's up to you. Suffice to say that from July through December you will glow with fire, with intensity of heart, and with physical energy and courage. (You're almost always courageous anyway.) If you're a male, females will melt when you come near. If you're a female Aries, pluck a man from whatever life he's living — you have the grit, the assertiveness and the sexual magnetism to hunt and land almost anyone you set your sights on. (Though I recommend suave, gracious men, or naive but energetic men.)

Speaking generally, Libra, Leo and Sagittarius are your best loves, with Aquarius and Gemini not far behind. From July to December, a Libra could be VERY interested — and frustrated? Depends on you.

CAREER / BUSINESS:

For your career, Aries, 2020 will be the worst of times, and the best of times, to quote Dickens. In macro terms, the three years ahead, 2020 through 22, will nudge you into a social-career "crossover" — golf with the boss, career seminars or conventions, etc. Your progress will, in the broadest ways, depend on your ability to make friends, especially with co-workers.

Almost all year (to mid-December) the planet of great good luck travels through your career, status and ambition sector. Good — great! But until May 5, the lunar south node does the same, and this node usually brings bad karma, subtle traps and unforeseen obstacles. Unfortunately, karma is stronger than luck, so caution flags continue to fly in this area — but it's all better than 2019, which was generally very "heavy" in career matters, sometimes too heavy to lift.

The main danger to your ambitions January to early May is, believe it or not, over-optimism (and its result, over-expansion). You might be tempted/persuaded to charge ahead, to push your ideas/proposals on higher-ups, to (like Roger Stone did) laugh in the face of the presiding judge. Well, never laugh at a judge, but as for pushing proposals and charging ahead — expect dangers here before mid-May, and superb success late May to December. For example, you could campaign for and land a juicy promotion in, say, March — then slowly find, as the years pass, that your promotion has put you in a dead-end, or given you incompatible duties. One other bit: DO NOT change careers, employers or jobs before May 5. It would be better to quit than change.

Bosses, parents, even judges will be temperamental mid-February through March. Be diplomatic, long-suffering, and quick to fix things — and keep your sense of humour. (Not, perhaps, in the boss' face.) Mid-May through June, head office or a gov't department might work against you, or bring to light your vulnerabilities — oops, forgot to file 2017's taxes?

The last seven months of 2020 do not contain these dangers — and in fact are the luckiest seven months, career-wise, in a 13-year cycle! Now, the cosmos urges you plunge in and charge ahead. Talk to higher-ups, parents and VIPs. Submit proposals, ask for higher responsibilities, display your skills — you're going up!

Remember one thing: your career environment is very "sober" this year (as it was in 2019) and also deeply linked to hidden factors, secret actions, financial, debt and investment areas, research and commitment (from 2008-2024). (These "secret actions" can be by other people.) There is a treasure chest here, hidden deep: dig and find it. Could be as simple as accepting equity (shares) from your employer as part of your pay package.

Bosses might be impatient and temperamental mid-February through March, so exercise diplomacy. (This is when you might be most tempted to push your favourite proposal — with very "uncertain" consequences!)

Work mates treat you affectionately in October. As this is also a relationship month, singles among you might begin a co-worker love affair. (Not one for the ages, as your sexual confidence flags this autumn.)

HOME / FAMILY:

Your domestic arena remains supportive, mellow and peaceful until May, Aries. The first four months are a superb time to make long-range decisions around your home, children, security, even your (eventual?) retirement. (Decisions you make now, and projects you start, will have a beneficial effect for at least 17 years.) Choose the children's school(s) and/or start an education fund. (Check with your gov't — many will contribute some sort of matching dollars.) Great time to start renovations/repairs/decoration, EXCEPT February 16 to March 9. (If started then, expect expensive mistakes.)

You can spend fortunately on luxuries — e.g., expensive furniture, wall art, plush carpets, quality clothes for the kids — mid-March to early April.

Lots of running around the neighbourhood April/May — don't lose your partner in the crowds!

May to December removes the domestic protection and family wisdom/peace of January-May. No serious problems follow, though.

A secret, or a gov't order, might be like a pebble in your shoe mid-May through June. Be patient, get regular periods of rest — July also.

Discuss family affairs in June/July — this period might delay domestic progress or bring a "missing" relative back. (DO NOT start a domestic project June 16 to July 11.)

July is very "home bound," yet sends you all over town visiting, yakking, buying little doo-dads. Despite the "sleepiness" of July, your energy and intensity (when awake!) is top-notch in late July and, especially, August. August is a beautiful month to decorate, landscape, paint, etc.

From September to December, not much affects your domestic sphere.

FINANCES / INVESTMENTS / DEBT:

You have two money sectors in 2020, Aries. On the earnings side, weekly pay check, client income, purchases and sales, all depend on your social skills. You will feel optimistic about this "short money" zone for 6 more years — and optimism is halfway to grand results!

I'm not guaranteeing grand results, as much depends on your response to the new, unpredictable and "electric" influence on your income.

The internet, AI, IT, electronics, electricity, social groups, NGO's, humanitarian and unusual, unique talents — any of these can be a road to better earnings in 2020.

Your earnings level will also respond favourably to your social activities. Earnings (etc.) will be favoured all year, and more in March, May and September/October. The second money area involves deep, invested money, property, land, assets, appreciation and growth. Here are your stocks and bonds, your retirement fund, etc. Here, few influences have any say this year. A potential partnership might arise in October, then stumble, then return in November/December.

HEALTH:

Note: I am not a doctor, so these comments are general, and do not necessarily apply to you.

You always need to protect your head, Aries. This year (and the next few) your nerves improve. Health concerns probably centre on your teeth/gums, bones, knees and skin (until 2025). Your career success (or lack of) can affect your health, especially in April and October. If you need it, hospitals or spas will welcome you with kindness and care. Overall, a good health year!

TAURUS

April 20 – May 20

Start nothing significant or important:
February 16 to March 9
June 18 to July 12
October 13 to November 3.

GENERAL:

Your beliefs will be very prominent in 2020, Taurus. This is an exciting, perhaps stressful year, as it "wakes you up" and injects a new vitality and ambition. This is a great year to pursue intellectual and cultural goals: university, foreign travel, statistics/insurance, fame, publishing, cultural and religious or philosophical involvements, legal and love matters. Until May 5, many of these wear "reversible jackets." In other words, you might meet success in these activities before May, but success might also hide a subtle trap. Be patient and time your actions for May onward, rather than earlier, as the luck in these legal, intellectual and international zones lasts all year. Strictly avoid lawyers and lawsuits before May 5 — you have a good chance of winning them after that date.

July through December, be careful not to make enemies, physical or "political" Avoid sunburn, sudden temperature changes, bumping your head, places of violence and belligerent people. Athletes among you might excel during these six months. The gov't might be your "constant companion" — taxes? regulations? restrictions? — during this last half of 2020. Make sure those civil servants will be in touch with you for a good reason, not a bad one. (I.e., behave!) You might, July to December, find a job position in administration or gov't.

Love will fill many of your days. (When doesn't it?) Your ruling planet, Venus, retrogrades in May/June, bringing you to a halt while you make some important decisions about money…and perhaps about an intimate "opportunity." For you, romance can pop up any month, and any year.

Until 2025, you look on life with optimism and deep wishes. Socializing, entertainment/fun, wish fulfillment and light romance weave a lovely streak through your life. You like spiritual or psychic friends, and these will come. (If single, you might even marry one.)

LUCK:

"Luck" is always of two kinds: the normal, daily or monthly luck that Jupiter (optimism and great worldly luck) and Venus (sweet love, attractions, and mild but good luck). And "karma," the ongoing result of actions we took and patterns we started and wove in the past, that now is rewarding us, or wrapping us in the punishing, restricting web of our own actions/consequences.

Jupiter:

This lucky planet will spend 2020 in Capricorn, your sign of intellect, higher learning, international affairs, law, publishing, statistics, insurance, far travel, love, and cultural, religious and philosophical beliefs. These sectors yield huge benefits in 2020, but read "Karma" below.

Jupiter is the wedding planet, and it spends all year (well, to December 19) in your sign of weddings — good news for single Taureans. To some degree, these activities (travel, wedding, higher learning, etc.) are fortunately connected to money, investments, or growth of assets. For instance, you might get a better return investing in foreign stocks than in those of your own nation.

Venus:

You are considered one of the luckier signs, Taurus, because your ruler is Venus, planet of affection, mild good luck, luxuries and ease. Venus favours you mid-January to mid-February, March (especially!) August (light, friendly affection) and October (romantic). From late November to mid-December, Venus will introduce single Taureans to a potential life mate. Late December, Venus nudges you toward the boudoir. Married folk might be celebrating a pregnancy this month. Earlier, Venus spends April to early August (4 months) in Gemini. This indicates a strong emphasis on earnings and casual/sensual sensual attractions.

You might need to mull over a (probably good) "merging" of your physical charms with someone's assets. Better results if you decide/act on this by late June, not before.

Karma:

With your lunar north node in Cancer until May, and your south node in Capricorn during the same time, the first 4 months will bless your quick, daily travel, business, communications and casual contacts, but warns you away from the "long side" of these — far travel, law, higher education, publishing, etc. For example, it will be far better to read a newspaper than a book. Better to agree verbally than in writing. These "long side" interests are actually lucky, but far luckier after May 5, when the dark cloud of karma does not hover over them.

From May to December, Your karmic areas to avoid are lust, investments, lifestyle changes, surgery and medical procedures, research, commitment and consequence. (You should have jumped on these in 2019, when they were super-lucky.)

Do not take advice from Sagittarians. During the same 8 months, you will find a smooth, calm, productive path if you accept surface appearances and stay on the lighter side of sex, money, and activities. So, do indulge casual sex, but reject deep sex, esp. extra-marital temptations.

Do buy and sell, chase earnings, but buy things that fall in value over time (car, groceries) and avoid investments (things that you hope will increase in value over time).

DO seek advice from Gemini people.

LOVE:

I wrote too much about love in the "Luck-Venus" section (above). But there's something to add:

2020 is one of the best love years in a decade. Last year attractions were primarily sexual. In 2020, love "ascends" to a gentle, socially-welcomed, compassionate and wise level — often, for singles, this translates into a wedding. For this reason, love is more important than usual.

The months listed as fortunate in your "Luck-Venus" section will be smooth and pleasant for lovers and spouses.

But love is most blessed, especially renewed love, and in a light, friendly way, February to early April.

As mentioned, you could grow indecisive about an attraction or lover; this might arise from a suspicion that your own feelings are too casual, not passionate enough. On the plus side, it's a good situation. More deeply, you are undecided about yourself (which causes any relationship indecision). Your present "world" is being shaken up, in unpredictable ways. But until the dust settles, perhaps you're wise to delay commitment. You'll reach a decision by July, but not before.

Romance can blossom very quickly and strongly late August and early September. November/December might bring a potential life-mate — but it's quick, and you'll need to act fast.

International travel, higher education, libraries and law offices will boost your romantic chances all year — perhaps in ultimately disappointing ways before May 5, and in deep, harmonious, gentle and — it's like your heart's being carried on a gentle breeze — May 5 to December.

CAREER / BUSINESS:

The years to 2026 will imbue you with some of the most powerful ambitions of your life, and, almost as a subconscious result, will spark career-related events, many of them quite pleasing. These years bring benefits if you socialize in your career. Friends equal not only advancement, but also a happy career.

December 2019 offered a chance to sweeten your prospects; you could spend much of 2020 developing or furthering an idea or contact which/who came to you in December 2019. This idea might involve higher education, languages, international travel or affairs, publishing, law, statistics or insurance — all areas that are blessed in 2020, mostly May onward. (Before May, be cautious with these, don't plunge in too early. If you do, you might set up circumstances that eventually oppose your goals.)

From January through mid-February, don't be impulsive with investments, the gov't, commitments or major changes. (In February, investments and gov't benefit you if you act thoughtfully and graciously.)

Mid-February through March, strictly avoid lawsuits — even lawyers. Higher-ups might be temperamental and impatient April to mid-May, so keep your sense of humour. An affair or flirtation might take you away from your ambitions in March.

Your earnings potential soars April to early August — an unusually lengthy period, marked by indecision or delays (in money) in May/June. Quietly campaign for a pay raise before May, then pursue one assertively July/early August. (Same period, April-August, is good for raising your prices, if you're in business.) February (remember, some small caution) June and October will be your strongest career months, in terms of solid hard work.

Oddly enough, Mercury's three 2020 retrogrades occur in these three months, bringing delays and indecision. This hints that many of you will be reconsidering your career or business this year — are you in the right one? Adjustments needed?

One thing's for sure: a freshness and new, shiny horizons, imbue your career prospects from 2019 to 2026. It can be stressful, so buckle up and charge ahead. Involvement will reduce stress; inactivity will exacerbate it. Final note: you're going places, but take a long view: 2020 is merely preparation for 2021, when your career prospects will soar with great luck!

HOME / FAMILY:

Your home and family are pretty well yours to shape in 2020, Taurus. No overwhelming influence, good or bad, affects you in this zone. Your domestic scene can be a little scrappy in early January, and stressful in late January/February (mainly because you're tied up with ambitions, impatient with "security") and November (some opposition?).

In general, your home will tend to run itself now to 2026. Your commitments and chores/burdens will lighten. This is not the best time to chase pregnancy, as you will be so "wired" to your outside ambitions. (Yet the chances that you will gain a step-child or adopt, rise significantly.)

Many background developments can occur from July to December — a family skeleton might be exposed, or you begin a major repair/renovation project, or must comfort a family member. These "background" area/activities might conflict with love and practical goals, especially August to October. If this happens, choose/favour love and practical demands.

Decoration projects and furniture purchases (or similar) lure you in February, but you'll be prone to mistakes. Though you might not see the mistake for some time, even months later, it can be costly. Instead, save these actions for late July and August.

A big garden party would be a great success, late July through September.

FINANCES / INVESTMENT / DEBT:

"Flowing money" — earnings, purchases, etc. — are blessed from April to early August. These are great months to ask for a pay raise, hold garage sales, seek bargains, schmooze with potential clients, etc.

Stable or static money — investments, net worth, assets, debts — should have risen in value last year (2019) but will tend toward inertia in 2020. This isn't a bad thing. It's more like a rest, a breather. If you do invest or adjust your holdings, April, August and December will tend to offer the best results. February, June and October, also usually good financial months, are impacted by indecision or delays.

International stocks/companies or projects offer fortunate investment prospects.

HEALTH:

Note: I am not a doctor, so these comments are general, and do not necessarily apply to you.

Your neck often is the source of health problems, Taurus — often, just a "stiff" neck. (Your neck is like a sensor — it grows stiff when you're tense, or ignoring a problem in other areas of life.)

In 2020, stress, jangly nerves, are your biggest potential physical problem. Start now — meditate, exercise in nature, garden, or ask your MD for relaxation techniques. (Television increases stress.) Like Aries, a lot of your health can be boosted up or impacted down by your career progress.

Your critical health planet (lucky Jupiter) spends 2020 in good, benign aspect to you all year, so you should be in good shape, especially from May onward.

Before May, take care in foreign countries (e.g., tainted fruit/water). Weight gain possible.

GEMINI

May 21 – June 20

Start nothing significant or important:
February 16 to March 9
June 18 to July 12
October 13 to November 3.

GENERAL:

2019 was a year of exploration or relocation, exciting meetings, possible life-mate surprises (a mate for singles, a separation for unhappy couples) — and opportunities. You were public, visible, even very opinionated!

2020 steers you into quieter — yet more potent — waters. What was more public, more open, now seeks shade, and grows deeper, yielding intimacy in love, funding in business. This is the best year in many for investing, reducing debt, solving a medical problem, changing your life style, getting pregnant, simply having sex, investigating or researching. BUT timing is important: before May 6, many of these activities can possess a hidden side, one that can restrict, burden, or even dead-end you as time passes.

So plan, ponder, research before May, and act mid-May onward, to December.

2020 isn't the most social of years, but it contains one massive social, popularity, dream-come-true optimism and flirtation period, spanning the entire second half. Old flames are very likely to appear (or you're likely to chase them) at various times during the year.

Surgery might occur to fix a long-standing problem. Try to avoid medical operations September to mid-November, when doctors can make mistakes.

You have struggled with temptation for some time, especially in sex and financial zones. By May, those temptations recede. This month starts an entire 18-month period in which you will be blessed, calm (relatively!) and wise. Give advice to others, as yours is accurate now (May 2020 to January 2022).

In legal, love, far travel and intellectual areas (2018 to 2026) you can feel un-assertive, or you might let things slide into "benevolent neglectful chaos." Try to keep files, gov't demands, correspondence in order.

It's a good year, Gemini — you are emerging from opposition, and "climbing" to reach one of the peaks of your life (2022). Your career and "standing" has been buoyant for the last 8 years — this continues in 2020.

LUCK:

"Luck" is always of two kinds. One the normal, daily or monthly luck that Jupiter (optimism and great worldly luck) and Venus (sweet love, attractions, and mild but good luck). And "karma," the ongoing result of actions we took and patterns we started and wove in the past, that now is rewarding us, or wrapping us in the punishing, restricting web of our own actions/consequences.

Jupiter:

Most of your luck in 2020 will lie hidden — in secret places and rendezvous, in closed door discussions, financial actions/investments, health probes, and other more or less private situations. Dig deep, reject surface appearances: treasure lies below. You will likely find it easy, this year, to attract an intimate lover. Until May, your luck is uncertain here (see "Karma" below). But May onward to December, you can strike it rich, make lucky investments, have a love affair, and/or fortunately change your life-style, perhaps your entire life. Let your key word for good fortune be: "changes." Your luck might slow mid-May to mid-September — that's okay, be patient. (Use these month for preparation, re-examining plans, etc.).

Venus:

This is everyone's planet of mild good fortune, and your own planet of love and romance. If you're a parent, this planet blesses your children and their development (skills, emotional openness, etc.)

Venus supports true love (and empathy, understanding) the first half of January. The last half, it touches your bosses with the wand of tolerance and affection — toward you. Venus brings friends and new hopes in February, and could strike love sparks. (Remember, 2020 is one of the sexiest year you've encountered in a while.) This planet aids relationships with bureaucrats, gov't and head office in March.

From April to early August, Venus sits in Gemini. This means several things: 1) you'll be the focus of many wandering, hopeful eyes; others will treat you with affection; your physical and deportment charms will glow; and 2) an important romance might visit singles (why does Aries keep popping up?); and 3) you will undergo a Spring of Indecision (May/June) — not only about love, but also about children, creative projects and prospects, gambling (with life as well as in cards) sports, games, beauty, risk and pleasure

— and, ultimately, about your life. These 4 + months (April-August) should also benefit you in dealings/enquiries with gov't, the tax man, head office, agents, advisors and charities.

In September, Venus introduces you to new friends, perhaps sends you on a happy trip. This planet will sweeten your home life almost all October. She (Venus is female) helps you with love, then work/co-workers, then face-to-face situations, partnerships, etc.

Karma:

Until May 5, your "difficult" karma lies in the arena of large finances, investments, exploration, extra-marital affairs, unfamiliar boudoirs, research, surgery and medical procedures, lifestyle changes — everything listed above under "Jupiter" luck. All 2020, these areas are blessed with Jupiter's lucky wand, but until May, good luck and bad karma mingle, which can throw a subtle monkey wrench into everything, causing delays, temptations, over-reaching (e.g. taking on too big a mortgage) and eventually, perhaps, disappointment.

From mid-May to December, this karmic cloud lifts, and you should plunge into big, big things: investment, or a big research project, surgery, changing your address, etc. May to December, commitment will bring rewarding consequences.

January to May 5, to ride with good karma, stick with short, not long; with surface, not depths, casual understandings, not firm commitments.

From May 6 onward (deep into 2021) your "good" karma lies in independence. Others will be attracted because you will radiate a subtle form of goodness, peace and wisdom. People who lack these qualities can be powerfully drawn to you. Some of them might even fight you, for instance in a lawsuit, because subconsciously they use this as a form of attachment. (If anyone sues or threatens you May

2020 to January 2022, simply do nothing: don't respond. They will either go away, or "hang themselves.")

Although 2020 is a powerfully sexual year, from May onward you should be very slow to commit to another, to seek a mate, to marry or start co-habitation. In other words, dive into romance, sex, friendship, but not partnership. This applies to business partnerships also. (In 10 - 15 % of cases, someone who enters your life in 2020 as a prospective mate will be destiny, a gift from karma, but in 85 - 90 % of cases, he/she will be, for some reason, an unsuitable mate. How to tell the difference? The gift, the true love, will almost fall into your lap, and the relationship will grow swiftly from there, w/o delays. The false or "bad" love will meet all sorts of delays, telephone tag, inability to agree on a good date night. If you find yourself scheming and planning, be cautious — it's a bad sign.

May 2020 to January 2022 is not a good time to relocate, deal with the public, engage in lengthy negotiations, make enemies, seek fame, or sign agreements that tie you down. Despite these gloomy warnings, you'll be happy!

LOVE:

For additional Gemini love hints, read "Luck" above.

A year ago, one of your love planets, Uranus, moved into a quiet, restrictive zone, where it will stay until 2026. This tends to steer at least some of your love desires into quietude, a restful place or posture, and into secrecy. A Taurus could become very dear to you, and some Gemini-Taurus weddings will occur this year and the next few. A Libra, who usually sees you as the brain without sex appeal, will change his/her tone and could become physically attracted.

Many single Geminis met their future (or present) mate in 2019. Some of you will meet that person this year or next. Until May, sex will tempt yet largely elude you. May to December, sex will be very available — and fortunate.

Though 2020 is a very practical year for you, many smaller flowerings of romance occur, and two major romantic periods arrive, one late Spring, the other from Summer to January 2021.

Small stuff: the first half of January wakes your love senses, as someone quirky but inspiring beguiles you. January to mid-February brings intensity to all your relationships. Be co-operative, make love not war. February spells optimism about love, especially the light, flirty kind. Someone met in a group could become an amour.

April to early August brings the first significant love phase: you will be uber-attractive, you'll glow with an endless succession of good hair days. You will also be indecisive (May/June) perhaps because you have more than one woo-er? A Taurus or Libra person might figure prominently.

A powerful second love phase runs from July to year's end. Whereas April to August is sweet (melting hearts) the July to December period is lively, bouncy, friendly, lightly romantic, and brings a constant round of popularity, optimism, laughter and flirtations.

Good friends abound, and one of them, or your whole group, could introduce you to someone as quick-witted, active and restless as you — maybe more so! Remember one thing: the July-December person might feel more casual toward you than you feel toward him/her.

So if a love affair starts during this period, keep it light until you know where you stand.

All year, you might form a life-bond based primarily on physical attraction. Give this time, wait to see other sides of the relationship (how do you communicate? shared interests? both parties gentle and supportive? If no sex, would you still "love?") before you become deeply involved. Forming a bond largely based on sex is a dangerous path January to April, but might actually be a fortunate way to start a broad-based romance, especially from May to December.

From early May to 2021, as noted earlier, be slow to form a hard commitment (wedding, co-habitation, etc.).

CAREER / BUSINESS:

Your career progress has been boosted since 2011/12, and will continue "upward" until 2025. In 2020, you will be valued for your insights, financial acumen, research/investigative abilities, and "soft power" (ability to sway others with a look, attitude or friendly persuasion). You will be most rewarded/promoted on the career scene if you're sympathetic, understanding and just.

Your peak career year of this early century will be 2022. Now to then, you will climb steadily higher. 2020 is a great year to start your own business — AFTER May 5. (Also, something you start May to December, can rebound to your career/status benefit down the road [2023-25].)

Bosses, judges, VIPs and parents favour you mid-January to early February. But don't let an intense relationship throw you off course, or sully your image in front of higher-ups. Walk away from fights before they start. Lots of talk and new career ideas/directives in February — but you ultimately hit indecision here. Avoid new (career) starts mid-February to March 10. Despite this indecision, higher-ups will load more responsibility on you than usual. (You'll finally make those decisions — correctly — later in March.)

May brings dealings and communications with head office, civil servants, or institutions. You're starting to make friends with these types.

Higher-ups display impatience and temperament mid-May through June — be diplomatic, smile! This "friction" will, oddly, be accompanied by wishes and hopes about your career — which a boss might grant.

In some ways, you will be on your own, or independent, in career, from May into early 2021. You grow indecisive about your tasks in October. Be patient, rather than leap too soon, or while you're still confused. Dive into work in November — get it done. December — opportunities.

HOME / FAMILY:

2020 is not really a down-home year, Gemini.

Friction might flare with your spouse January/February — try saying "yes, dear" 100 times. Despite your awakened ambitions, you might be tied to a) a back-room project, or b) home sweet home, in March and May. July starts with indecision, but by mid-month onward you can buy items for the home — furniture, paint, etc.

Home and family will be a place of many discussions (and running around the 'hood) late August to early September. Use your home to gain deep rest in May and September. The family will be sweet, comforting in October.

In December, you and your spouse might say: should we travel? And off you go. 2020 favours investing in any form AFTER May 5. This opens the door to buying a home, which isn't a bad idea.

FINANCES / INVESTMENT / DEBT:

This area is probably the most important — holds the greatest dangers and greatest rewards — of 2020. The dangers await you January to May 5. You can easily avoid them by not investing, not making huge financial moves. It's always good to clear debts, but don't clear them so drastically before May that you leave yourself with no "room to move."

From May to December, the dangers dissolve, and rewards take their place. During this period, you can safely and profitably invest in almost anything — home or real estate, stocks and bonds, commodities, or your own business. This is also a good time to tell the boss you would rather receive stock than a pay raise.

Jump on an opportunity January 18/19. (18 if you live in North/South America.) You need to avoid impetuous investing mid-February through March — you're being too optimistic! April's interesting but "produces poverty." In March and May, the gov't might provide a grant or "free" loan

— seek, ask, apply. Be careful with money decisions mid-June to mid-July — better to wait until the second half of July, when your mind is clear, instincts sharper. September invites you to invest in a new home or other real estate (or in premises for a business). Your friends might advise against a financial action in October/November — they're very probably wrong.

HEALTH:

Note: I am not a doctor, so these comments are general, and do not necessarily apply to you.

Your lungs and nervous system are your most vulnerable sides, Gemini. (You might be most nervous in February, May, August, and November.) If you do smoke, try to quit now. (2020 is a great year for changing habits and lifestyle factors.)

Deep, serious health is a bit of a puzzle now: on the one hand, the planets ruling sexual diseases, teeth/gums, bones, knees and skin are in your critical health zone now — but the one ruling all these except sex, will leave your health sign this Spring (then return Summer onward, to leave "permanently" in December — good news!). Until May, any health problems can expand quickly, so get to a doctor at the first signs of trouble. May to December, your health should improve — perhaps in lucky ways.

Surgery might occur to fix a long-standing problem. Try to avoid surgery September through mid-November, when doctors can make mistakes. ("Surgery" includes laser and ultrasound procedures.)

CANCER

June 21 – July 22

Start nothing significant or important:
February 16 to March 9
June 18 to July 12
October 13 to November 3.

GENERAL:

2020 is a year of huge opportunities for you, Cancer — but the really valid ones will come early May to December, NOT earlier. Earlier, many "opportunities" are really prison doors, tying you up in problems and obstacles, and shutting you off (because you're so busy with the false opportunity) from real, splendid openings.

Before May, you face the same situation or relationship environment as in all 2019 — tempting prospective partnerships, which will tend to end, if you embrace them, with confusion, alienation, lack of production, and ultimate disappointment. During this first part of the year, be independent, a self-starter.

The entire year expands opportunities and partnership prospects (love or business) but before May you will likely be too optimistic, and could embrace the very thing (or person) who would defeat or work against you.

From May 5 onward, relationships, relocation, fame, public dealings, negotiations, contracts, life-mate kind of love — these expand in major, beneficial ways. If single, you could meet your life-mate. This "expansion" also affects enmities, litigation/court fights, etc. — so be happy, cheerful, friendly and philosophical — and diplomatic! (If anyone sues you before May, ignore them — they'll tend to hang themselves. If you get down in the mud with them, that's where you'll be — in mud.

Many single Cancers will wed, or meet true love/true mates, especially May to mid-December.

From July to year's end, your career shows two features: one, your soaring ambition, and two, irritable bosses. Humour them (and step on no toes) and you could shoot up ambition's ladder.

A new kind of friend (indeed a new, livelier and unpredictable social life) started to enter your life in 2019. These friends are a bit quirky or nerdy, quick, very friendly (everyone's their friend) and erratic — and loyal, though sometimes it will be hard to find them.

This trend continues — and grows stronger — now to 2026. In 2020, especially January, you might make a friend who turns out to be a superb intimate or financial partner.

Your mind and your intuition are hard to tell apart from 2011 to 2025. Your ideas are good, you might even be asked to teach. An international voyage (especially a sea cruise) calls you all year. Far travel, and any intellectual journey, will enhance your spiritual side. Now to 2025, you can see how one gets to heaven.

LUCK:

"Luck" is always of two kinds: the normal, daily or monthly luck that Jupiter (optimism and great worldly luck) and Venus (sweet love, attractions, and mild but good luck). And "karma," the ongoing result of actions we took and patterns we started and wove in the past, that now is rewarding us, or wrapping us in the punishing, restricting web of our own actions/consequences.

Jupiter:

Jupiter, planet of great good luck, spends almost every day of 2020 in your sector of relationships, relocation, fame, public dealings, negotiations, contracts, life-mate kind of love — and of opposition or co-operation, negotiation or litigation, fame or notoriety, love or war. From May to December, your best outcome will occur when you partner, co-operate, or "go out to the other." Others hold the luck, the aces, all year — you advance by jumping on their train. BUT you probably remember that I'd advised, all 2019, to avoid partnerships and binding commitments. This advice continues into the first 4 months of 2020. Yet Jupiter is saying, "Leap, the water's fine!" My advice until May 5: consider leaping, study the situation, prepare, plan, but don't leap before May. And if a different opportunity or relationship prospect shows itself after May 5, jump into this new one, and abandon your pre-May goals/plans. The world is fresh, and you could face a new life, new love, soon!

Venus:

Venus is the planet of love, but for you it focuses that love into two areas: home and kids, and friends and social groups. Venus will spend a significant portion of 2020 — April through July — in your "inner world" zone. During these 4 months, you will re-examine your home/family and your social connections. You'll see mistakes to clear up, past rudenesses, etc. During this period, work to heal and regrow your faith in humanity and life. Meditate — the spiritual realm favours you. So, too, do institutions, admin. workers, civil servants, advisors and agents, these 4 months. True friends will not only stick with you, they'll affectionately aid you.

Venus brings a sweet, mellow understanding in January. She aids your ambitions in February, makes higher-ups favour you. In March she brings friends. April to August she heals your soul — and gov't-type contacts. Most of August she makes you appealing to the opposite sex. In September, she brings you money. In October, happy friends and pleasant journeys. November, domestic joys, sweet children. December, romance and friendly co-workers — a workplace romance?

Karma:

Until May 5:   Your "bad karma" lies in relationships and environment. To fail, chase new bonds, relocate, marry, form a business or other partnership, jump on "opportunities," seek a centre of gravity outside yourself. Same period, your "good karma" will roll out a smooth, productive path if you remain essentially independent and self-directed. (E.g., stay married, but view your spouse's advice/projects a bit skeptically.) These 4 months are one of the wisest periods of your life, so make long-term decisions now, especially about relationships.

After May 5:   The karmic picture changes dramatically: everything that I advised against before May 5, now becomes not only fortunate, perhaps very fortunate, but wise too: relocation, marrying, partnering, jumping on opportunities, fame or dealing with the public, negotiations and agreements — all these hit a decade height of promise and reward.

Now disappointment and endless obstacles face you if you give too much time and effort to "hands-on" work. May to December (and actually to January 2022) advises against machinery purchases, hiring employees, new pets, and letting your children enslave you.

("Mommy, Mommy, Mommy!")

But you will succeed this May-December if you work in an administrative, management role, delegate tasks, attend policy and closed-door meetings, meditate and ponder, welcome a spiritual influence, and deal with agents, civil servants and advisors. This is particularly so May to early August, when you could be surprised at the gov't's largesse.

LOVE:

Love this year, for singles, is heavily weighted toward marriage or co-habitation. You singles could meet true love, even your destined life mate. But read "Luck" under "Jupiter" and "Karma" for the January to May 5 period — your best meetings, attractions and heart developments will arise May to December. Both your marriage and romance planets spend the year in your marriage sector — an exciting, destined "merging" looks likely! Realize the one for you will be diplomatic, inscrutable, sexually oriented, ambitious and stubborn. You might have to be a little flexible, accepting.

You married Cancers will face many ups and downs, perhaps struggles, with your partners. If you are in a lifeless or unhappy marriage, 2020 can end it — guilt free, because your partner wants freedom as much as you do. If you are happily married, 2020 (especially after April) brings adventure, a boost in socializing, and a lot of teasing and laughter.

Bright new friends enter all Cancer's lives from 2019 to 2026. These people are unpredictable, eccentric free spirits — here today, gone tomorrow (and back on Wednesday). Despite the unpredictable behaviour, these are very loyal people. Some of these friends will attract you in a deeply sexual way, and you could jump into an affair — not a good idea if you're married.

The intellectual and cultural side of love is blossoming these years (2012-2025) — many Cancers who do fall in love will wed — many more than usual. Your love prospects rise if you travel internationally (including cruises) attend higher learning, or haunt libraries, court rooms, lawyers' offices, and/or transportation hubs. Your "true love" might be foreign-born.

January is for peer-to-peer relationships, but you are also buried in work demands and career ambitions, so love gets little time. But late month, into February, your sexual side awakens and a sweet, perhaps secret, intimacy starts. Late February into March, you become indecisive about love — especially about its meaning, its long-range viability, acceptance of a union by others…These doubts clear by late March, April.

Your lust grows intense April through mid-May, could involve someone on your work or career scene. It progresses: social, friendly, then intimate. You face many doubts — and a breather — involving your home, May/June. You might frame a new love in domestic terms, to "foresee" what marriage would be like with this person. Someone might pursue you assertively May/June (and in an odd way, mentally, or with "profound" conversation) but you grow indecisive, right into mid-July.

You attract attention and get your way in July and much of August — that can apply to love, also. September's for friends and a home party. In October, you or someone might be sending love hints, romantic notes or calls. By mid-month, though, this person (or you) withdraws, delays. That's okay — by November indecision ends and a green love light shines. December has a bit of romance early, but is mostly a work month.

CAREER / BUSINESS:

In general, your career and practical ambitions face three large trends:

1) All year (but better May to December) "opportunity" is your key
word — chase new agents and/or clients, jump through open
doors, be willing to relocate for your career, form working
partnerships, deal with the public, negotiate. You could land on
golden shores — a pay raise, new title, enhanced status — but
remember, "accept" these until May, then assertively chase
these, May onward.

A slow-down might occur mid-May to mid-September, but this is not
unlucky — instead, it's a great time to scan options, plan, ponder
outcomes, research and prepare — then launch yourself September
onward. (December is good for work, accomplishing, and
Machinery.)

2) July to December intensifies your career scene. Events are swift,
hectic. Be alert, lively and hard-working. Bosses are watching, and
they're impatient — delays will tell on their temper. (Same with
judges, if you're criminal or in a civil suit.) Be diplomatic, and retain
your sense of humour. Don't try to escape scrutiny — instead, realize
that, despite the "roughness" of higher-ups, this period can also shoot
you up ambition's ladder.

Listen, Cancer, do not make enemies, step on toes, nor compete with
or ignore higher-ups. You could rise! Take care early August and
October, when an opportunity and your boss's wishes, are in strong
conflict. (You might "break free" during this time, and set out on
your own.)

3) If you ask, you can receive a solid boost, even financial support
for your projects from gov't, large corporations or institutions from
April to early August. Avoid lawsuits, mid-May through June.
Launch an ambitious project July to September, or after mid-
November, not in-between.

HOME / FAMILY:

"Home is where the heart is" was probably penned by a Cancer. Your root, your very centre, lies in your home and family, even extended family. No major influences enter your domestic sphere in 2020, so the atmosphere will be calm overall, mellow and fruitful. You start 2020 with plans to change the home or garden. Workers and machinery can aid landscaping and renovations January to mid-February — but stop then, as February's second half and early March bring confusion, delays, mistakes and false starts. Don't start anything legal involving your home, family or property.

Your home, and generally any place, becomes a haven of retreat, or of good resting/pondering — a soul spa — April to August. A child might need extra care. Your family pampers and comforts you affectionately. Spend on your home in September. Exercise curiosity about your 'hood, make new contacts among the neighbours, in October. Home and outside ambitions vie for your attention this month — home's best. Your kids thrill you with their talents in November. December pulls you away from home — work, career call!

FINANCES / INVESTMENT / DEBT:

2021 will be your huge, lucky financial year. Spend 2020 planning and prepping for it, studying investments, working out a debt-reduction plan (if severe, visit one of those debt negotiators). In other words, keep your powder dry for next year, when huge, fortunate opportunities will arrive. A HUGE change in your financial picture will occur from 2021 onward for over a decade — prepare for this by getting your financial house in order, free up cash, eliminate debt, etc. The change could be a change of home, or a change of assets. Again, be ready.

2020 is quite fortunate if you invest in and/or start your own business. Luck-starred practical projects, projects demanding work and a bit of sacrifice, are available January to March, and again July to December. (From July through September, reprise a project from the past — even from the Spring.) These projects have solid long-range prospects, could grow fruitfully for decades. (They might be the genesis of those big changes arriving from 2021 to 2042.)

Your investment planet moved into Taurus a year ago, and will stay there until 2026. This hints that 1) you will be continuously optimistic about your assets and worth; and 2) your financial growth will be inextricably tied to your friends, social group — and, most importantly, to your ability to befriend others, and to bravely follow your optimism about investments.

If investing or financially re-arranging in January/February, when you're prone to, STOP by February 14.

HEALTH:

Note: I am not a doctor, so these comments are general, and do not necessarily apply to you.

Your health vulnerabilities usually centre on your breasts, womb, and stomach, Cancer. (And these "areas" in men.) Generally, your health should be quite good now, especially the first four months of 2020. Your health seems to be tied to relationships. And this year, after May, relationships blossom with good fortune. But late March through June, and again December into 2021 and 22, your relationship planet moves into your sex and critical health sector. (So if you're sexually adventurous, keep condoms handy.)

This Spring can bring hardenings: gall stones, bone spurs, etc. Before this possibility occurs, try a preventive diet.

From May onward, niggling health irritations occur, the kind that you can alleviate with over-the-counter cures. Watch weight gain on your hips.

LEO

July 23 – August 22

Start nothing significant or important:
February 16 to March 9
June 18 to July 12
October 13 to November 3.

GENERAL:

2020 is a year of hard work, Leo. This work can benefit your career, and is a necessary step toward "being king" in 2023. 2020 is a splendid time — best in a decade — to purchase machinery, car or appliances, to seek employment or hire employees. You'll benefit if you take these actions from May to December. Before, January through April, be cautious, as every bargain, every opportunity, might be a gift-wrapped monkey wrench. You will tend to be creative in your work — more so, in 2020.

From 2019 to 2026, your career, neighbourhood reputation and worldly status will be vibrant, unpredictable (with sudden events) and change-prone. You might not be in your present career in a few years. Much will depend on your ability to persuade others to co-operate, join.

You are the archetypal romantic, Leo, but from 2011 to 2025 you seem to be drawn more toward sex than romance. The exception was last year, 2019, when very significant romance might have filled your heart with song and thrill. Keep this amour going, but realize work and health concerns might create some "dry spells" in love's weather. By 2021, this romance (or another) can lead to marriage.

Your health needs some care this year, particularly in areas of teeth, gums, knees, bones and skin. Try solutions before May, but don't over-apply medicines. It's a good time to take blood tests, to check viral elements and platelets, and stress levels.

In money and growth of assets, 2020 is an open field. Your earnings and investment growth should expand, but it's up to you — make the effort, and you'll succeed.

Far travel and intellectual pursuits are "crowded" by work demands, but they do enter a significant cycle, July to year's end. In the September to November portion of this, delays and indecision can mar far travel, cultural and intellectual events, social rituals, media and broadcasting interests. so start projects in these zones before September, or after mid-November. Also, July to year's end, avoid lawsuits.

LUCK:

"Luck" is always of two kinds: the normal, daily or monthly luck that Jupiter (optimism and great worldly luck) and Venus (sweet love, attractions, and mild but good luck). And "karma," the ongoing result of actions we took and patterns we started and wove in the past, that now is rewarding us, or wrapping us in the punishing, restricting web of our own actions/consequences.

Jupiter:

This planet of great good fortune spends 2020 in your sector of work, health, dependents and tools/machines. You'll find it easy to get a job. (Or, if you're a boss, it's a good time to hire.) This is the kind of year in which your boss would rather promote you than let you quit. Jupiter also expands whatever it touches. So if a health problem occurs, get to the doctor before it grows. You will be tempted to spend a lot on machinery — good.

Venus:

Venus rules love, but for you specifically, it governs career/status/ambitions and communications/travel. This decade (2019-26) your partnership planet, Uranus, slowly travels through one of these Venus signs, which can impel you to marry "up" during these seven years. You might meet someone stunningly attractive in your career environment in March and October. (But hopefully not before March 8, unless she/he is a former flame.)

Venus helps you solve legal, travel and media issues in February. This planet will "crowd" your social life with new friends, and your plans with new optimism, from April to early August. A "lull" appears in the middle (May/June) during which two old friends from the past contact you, or you grow indecisive about loyalties. Venus imbues you with grace and charm in September — you'll attract followers! This planet sweetens your home late November/early December, and could spark an important romance (or casino win) in December.

Karma:

Until May 5, Leo, you will experience a smooth, mellow path when dealing with bureaucrats and civil servants, institutions (hospitals to universities) and charitable or spiritual organizations. To succeed, seek advice, agents. Rest deeply, and withdraw to plan. Delegate tasks, manage, and be alert to (or form) "policy." Be willing to undergo surgery or a brief hospital stay.

To fail before May 5, Leo, do the opposite: delegate nothing and do all the work yourself — "hands on." Trust no one else's skills. Try to cure serious health symptoms with herbs or over-the-counter remedies. Buy machinery or appliances.

After early May, everything changes: now your road to karmic peace and benevolence lies in social life, friends, popularity, optimism, and light, friendly romance (May to January 2022). Attend parties, seminars, conventions, join a political party, flirt, laugh and be witty. Embrace life's joy and goodness, and you'll win. Steer toward group creativity — e.g., work collaboratively on a film, rather than write a book alone.

But disappointment, dead ends and false starts will frustrate you May onward, if you dive into deep, heart-pounding, blushing romance. Avoid deep, independent creative or risky projects, beauty programs, decorating, teaching children (unless that's your job) and immediate or self-indulgent pleasure.

LOVE:

You're the great lover of the zodiac, Leo. There won't be a lot this year, as your work will expand to fill empty hours. Still, if you found love in 2019 it is very likely to survive (and 2021 brings a lucky marriage year).

Big picture, from May onward deep romance will disappoint, light romance will sail on happily.

Close up: January and the first half of February boosts romance, and will either re-ignite 2019's ardour, or spark a new one. You're sexually "awakened" mid-January to early February — and late February/March, perhaps by an old flame. Some of you will marry or co-habitate now.

April to mid-May, relationships intensify — make love, not war. Love is much more likely, as the same month, April, blesses your social life and brings an atmosphere of delight, fun, and flirtation — all the way to early August. You might mull over whether a love, or a social connection, will last, is real, should be embraced, in May/June. It's complicated, as your sexual desires flare strongly, both months. Co-workers tempt! An old friend/flame might appear these 2 months.

From July to year's end, someone might chase you. If so, he/she is bright, humorous, assertive verging on aggressive, and as enthusiastic about life as you are. This long period could bring a formal wedding, or even start a new love, a powerful one. Be wary mid-September to mid-November, when you don't have all the facts, and could make a mistake or wrong decision about someone. You attract others in August and September, when your physical charms shine. December is for true romantics!

CAREER / BUSINESS:

If I could label this section "Work," I could end this quickly: lots of lucky work! Your career (and status) are undergoing changes, 2019 to 2026. This will make relationships, partnerships, relocation, negotiations, dealings with the public, contracts, fame even, essential parts of your climb. Be ambitious, but also be other-oriented. Your social life (and skills) will soar benevolently April to August — use these to schmooze, mingle with higher-ups and prospective clients or co-operators, attend the company picnic, etc.

This is an excellent year to buy machines, tools and appliances — and to seek employment, and to hire others — all AFTER May 5. (Before this, be cautious: machines can be duds, or new employment, new employees, can disappoint in the long run.) May and August/September bring good buys, hires. Look at all factors in September, though — engines need thorough "vetting."

Your work/job expands in January, but is it taking you where you want to go? Maybe not. March might bring power-plays (best avoided — but realize higher-ups favour you in March). You're naturally ambitious in May, and might (in late April?) receive hints of a new career direction. July can drag you into closed-door meetings, policy and strategy discussions — speak, address such concerns after July 11, not before. (You'd have to retract.) You shine in August, of course — you do every August. Money comes in, September. Paperwork, travel, communications in October. November: slow down, take a wee rest.

The efforts you expend in 2020 will, if not sooner, pay off in a career "prize" about 2023.

HOME / FAMILY:

Overall, 2020 will be a mild, co-operative time in domestic affairs. Family members appreciate and support your work, although they sense your work and position are " changeable" — this might cause some trepidation, especially in late October, early November (and a bit, too, in late January, late may and late July). Respond by talking and hugging — you can truthfully say, "All's well."

March might have been a good down-home time, but you get called away, to, likely, a fortunate career effort. (Settle for spousal intimacy instead.) Late October into November really brings you home — rest, contemplate; but don't decorate or landscape or reno before November 2.

From 2009 to 2025, your home and work seem to meld together. This could have many of you working in real estate, or as tilers or carpenters of builders, farmers, homemakers (Oh, the chauvinism!) etc. It also favours working in a home office.

Home projects are best begun before April or after October 4. The period in-between is for 'scoping, planning, researching, etc.

FINANCES / INVESTMENT / DEBT:

You are in the middle of a long (2011-2025) and potentially very fruitful investment period, Leo. 2020 is no different, although it hints that your best investments this year will tend to be in machinery, tools, autos, manufacturing, medical appliances, mining (especially lead, silver or other metals of the same "colour") — anything that tends to "accompany" labour. (In fact, you could invest in hiring or "temp" firms and profit nicely.) Listen to your hunches and intuition all these years; they're "smarter" right now than logic. Your best investing times are before late June, and December.

Since you're probably gainfully employed all year, this is a good time to whittle down debt. Put a pre-determined portion of your pay check, say 20 %, to reduce debt.

Mid-January to early February offers rewarding financial moves. Research, dig deep for answers — they can be golden. Be careful about financial commitments mid-February to March 11 — deal with old or ongoing $ projects, reject brand new ones. (After the 11th, March is powerfully fruitful in finances.) Gov't programs or management support can come in March as well as July.

Mid-May through June could involve you in a legal-financial activity. This could manifest as a debt-reduction "court" proceeding, or can hint at investments in foreign countries, international firms, schools and academia, import-export, insurance, statistics/polling, publishing and similar concerns.

(Careful April and early May — a legal fight might occur, or a business "war" — or you could let your ideals lead you to $ loss — a good choice if you make it freely.) Earnings and income look good September/October. Depend on work as your main money source all year.

HEALTH:

Note: I am not a doctor, so these comments are general, and do not necessarily apply to you.

Your main organ is your heart, Leo — protect it always with moderate exercise and sensible eating habits. Now to 2026, stress can strain your heart, so do what you can to reduce it — meditation, nature walks, gardening, relaxation techniques. Television increases stress. Your lower back is often vulnerable, too — in exercise and work, follow the rules: lift without bending, etc. An ergonomic chair could

work wonders if you're a sit-down worker. Until May, your back, your bones, teeth/gums, skin and knees might need care. Even from May onward, a problem these areas can expand, and might need a doctor's advice.

VIRGO

August 23 – September 22

Start nothing significant or important:
February 16 to March 9
June 18 to July 12
October 13 to November 3.

GENERAL:

2020 is your year of great luck in romance, creative and speculative projects, beauty, art, immediate pleasure, and love of/raising children. The best developments in love will arrive mid-September onward, but the entire year excites.

This is also a stand-out year for two others things: career and worldly standing, and strong sexual and financial desires/occurrences. You can go to school now to improve your work performance and career prospects.

Higher-ups, parents, judges and VIPs favour you from April to early August, but you will face some indecision, too. A pay raise will be almost impossible to avoid! From May right into early 2022, your career and reputation will flow easily upward; but your home (and real estate) need caution.

From July to year's end, your sexual urges will grow or "dominate" as they haven't for 25 or so years. This can, of course, bring the physical side of love, during this major romantic year. If you're seeking pregnancy, it's available now. (Only danger: miscarriage, so test or remain alert for this.)

Your life can change in dramatic ways in 2020. Throughout, think deeply, research a potential major move/action before undertaking it.

Three times this year, Mercury, your ruling planet, retrogrades (seems to turn backwards relative to the Earth's speed and direction). These retros all occur in relationship signs for you — in your marriage/partnership house, then in your "happy friends and light romance" sector, and finally in your casual contacts zone. Notice how we start with intensity (marriage) and slowly devolve to mere casual contacts. These retros will be times of indecision, delays, possible false starts, and returning old flames. In other words, you will ponder your relationships all year.

You continue to be attracted yet frustrated by a special kind of person: quiet, shy, elusive, dreamy, psychic or intuitive, and basically non-rational. This is your "other side," your opposite — and maybe your mate.

Your mind will be alert and productive now to 2026. Same period, you will likely travel more than usual, and might be "drafted" for more intellectual work.

LUCK:

"Luck" is always of two kinds: the normal, daily or monthly luck that Jupiter (optimism and great worldly luck) and Venus (sweet love, attractions, and mild but good luck). And "karma," the ongoing result of actions we took and patterns we started and wove in the past, that now is rewarding us, or wrapping us in the punishing, restricting web of our own actions/consequences.

Jupiter:

Your 2020 arena of great good luck lies in creative and romantic zones, Virgo. You'll come off well in gambling venues, sports/games, decorating, playing with or teaching children, art and beauty, vacation and pleasure areas. This luck will be a little unreliable, or worse, before May 5, then super-duper May to mid-December.

Hopefully you got a lot of rest in 2019, because the good fortune of 2020 will keep you on your toes, and might involve helping someone move, sudden journeys (even international ones) or law, religion or higher education. Any of these can introduce you to a prospective lover.

Venus:

Venus is your planet of earnings and possessions, and of gentle love. (When I write "gentle love," I mean it's in the head, it's culturally and socially acceptable, and in some ways is a deeper — and certainly less selfish — love than the romantic kind. It's the kind of love that often ends in a wedding.) Venus favours you in January/early Feb., when it sweetens interactions between equals (e.g., your spouse). In February/early March, this planet heightens your sex drive, and fulfills it. (Yet, perhaps because intimacy is so sweet, so available, you begin to grow indecisive about this bond! My advice: wait it out. An old flame could appear. Marriage or co-habitation could occur.

April to early August, Venus persuades all above you — judges, parents, bosses — to look kindly on you, and to welcome your suggestions and proposals. This is a superb time to ask for a pay raise (before May, or better, after June 25). You could be promoted!

In September, Venus smooths, rewards your relations with head office or the gov't. In October, she renders you appealing, accents your physical appeal. Someone watches, wants. In November, Venus flows money your way, and helps you make a luxury purchase. In December, she blesses your home and family.

Karma:

Until May 5, Virgo, your "bad" karma lies in your romantic sphere — the same place that Jupiter blesses with great luck. But karma is stronger than luck. Luck is, in a sense, karma's tool or handmaiden. This counsels treating "heavy" or serious romance, creative and speculative projects, beauty, art, and opportunities for immediate pleasure — and raising children — with some caution.

To succeed before May 5, chase social or political groups, clubs of any kind, popularity, entertainment, and light, friendly romance. Envision the future, be optimistic, form wishes — these will guide you along a smooth, mellow and productive path.

After May 5, and right into early 2022, your good karma lies in your career zone — making this an excellent time to change careers or employers, to make lifetime decisions about your ambitions, and to work toward a promotion. Chase opportunities in the outside world

If you want to fail in 2020, want to meet disappointment down the road, then buy property or a home, seek security, withdraw, be humble, and avoid striving upward, avoid the "rat race." Garden, landscape, buy furniture, renovate, decorate. (This is hard for you, as you love gardens and nature.)

LOVE:

The best developments in love will arrive mid-September onward, but the entire year excites. Your main love (if you're not already attached) might be someone who you lived with, or who lived nearby, in the past (perhaps in 2019).

Your sexual urges surge from July to year's end. This blends with your huge romantic luck this year, but you can disrupt a romance if you push too hard for intimacy (or too weakly — just find the healthy midpoint). The danger of "pushing too hard" is strongest in early August and October.

Before May, stick with groups, socializing, and light, friendly romance. Deep, heart-filled passion will meet obstacles, delays, and might spur you to glom onto someone who, at core, wants freedom more than you. May to September can bring an old flame — maybe someone you lived with, or near to, in the past. Mid-September to year's end will tend to bring new love (unless of course you're already attached).

All year, and until 2026, a new element enters love on the mental side, surprising you with unexpected meetings (and splits) unusual, new ideas about wedded love, and a tendency to link love and work — for example, love with a co-worker. True love will continue to be: 1) very available, and 2) puzzling, because it's hard to understand this person, who is not logical, cares nothing for details, and works by intuition or dreaming. This to 2025. Same period, don't settle for someone who drinks or does recreational drugs excessively.

Best months for love: January (make sure you want what you chase) mid-February through March (sex drive high. but you — or he/she —are indecisive about commitment) May (bright, fresh, starts an intense face-to-face dynamic lasting through June — can be powerful sexually, but also can start a war!) July (light, friendly romance, hopeful joy) and September (when you're extra attractive).

CAREER / BUSINESS:

Your career undergoes one remarkable phase: from April to early August, parents, higher-ups, bosses, VIPs and judges favour you — really favour you. Use this time to push for a promotion, seek more responsibilities, and/or propose projects to the boss. (If you're a politician, this a "get elected" time.) However, be patient rather than push anything from May 12 to June 24, when your attempts to climb will get lost in the boss's indecision. (A career opening from the past might re-appear May/June — sure, grab it.)

February's filled with chores. You might be tasked with handling a budget, investments, or to research a higher-up's project. Those you work for are flush with money, so it's not a bad time to ask for a raise. March presents opportunities (and might entail relocation, at least temporarily). But before March 10, the only "real" ones are from the past. Work intensifies April/May — you might also get a glimpse of a new (more serious and more creative) work regimen to come in solidly from December (late) to 2023. Watch your health — eat, dress sensibly.

June puts your ambitions in the spotlight. Higher-ups are watching your performance. Don't let this "panic" you into ill-considered efforts — from May 13 to June 24, start no new, significant projects. Use all your energy to 1) support and protect ongoing ventures, and/or 2) reprise a project/association from the past. You'll get "good marks!"

Communicate with head office or civil servants, libraries or other information sources in August…and follow up a request in September. Ask for money in September/October. Bosses are no longer charmed by you, but your peers (especially those of the opposite sex) might be! November's for paperwork and short trips — again, a good opportunity to ask for a pay raise. In December, it's time to rest, to be with family and kids.

HOME / FAMILY:

Friction might mar your domestic scene in January/February. You can "water this down" if you turn your energy and determination to home-related projects such as landscaping, repairs, etc. Your spouse will soothe your heated brow by being extra sweet during most of these weeks.

If you are married, the whole year promotes pleasures at home, happy children, great vacation adventures and splendid results from painting, decorating, new furniture, bonfires and marshmallows, etc. If you're single, romance might be quickly followed by a new, twosome home. You might meet a prospective love near home, or during a house party or any domestic gathering. However, in both cases, be cautious about love relationships and pleasure before May.

From May to December (and beyond through 2021) your best time and best outcomes will not occur at home, but outside it — e.g., in career, higher education. DON'T buy real estate, nor change homes (unless unavoidable) after April. This is a poor time to change how you raise the kids, or their education plans/funds, etc.

December is a true "down home" month. The family is full of plans and discussions to mid-month, then of sweetness and affection the last half. December also "ends" 2020's romantic blessings, and brings the first shy green shoots of a new regimen — and good luck — in work, employment and health concerns.

FINANCES / INVESTMENT / DEBT:

From July to year's end, your investment planet roars back and forth in your investment sign (Aries). This is unusual, occurs perhaps every quarter-century. Other than your after-May romantic luck, this financial influence is the strongest theme of 2020. Invest — or re-arrange assets, or seek debt reduction — with forethought, not impulsively.

January/February can nudge you to invest in property, home items, and home-related companies, as well as in mining, forestry, and agriculture. Expect an average return. You might turn into a "gambling investor" in March. April/May brings a healthy income from work — use it to pay down debts. (Pay strict attention to safety regulations these two months.)

Foreign influences, international companies, import/export, and legal considerations impact your finances in July. This is the start of a six-month "financial adventure" which can raise you into riches, or at least can reduce debt. (August is the best month to visit a debt counsellor, or to ask the gov't to reduce a tax penalty, etc.) You'll end this half-year period with satisfaction, but almost sweating from the "high drama" of risking your funds.

Financial events in 2020 can affect your future in ways that change your lifestyle. One thing: don't be tempted to "buy sex" — trying to impress a date (or a marriage prospect) with your money/income/assets, is really buying sex.

HEALTH:

Note: I am not a doctor, so these comments are general, and do not necessarily apply to you.

Venereal diseases need caution July through December. Avoid banging your head, unsafe fire/heat, rashes and sudden temperature changes for these six months. Surgery might be called for — if so, it should proceed smoothly, and be very effective. As every year, protect your wrists and ribs. Your energy's low in August — rest deeply, for this lucky year demands much energy. From May onward, you need to watch your digestion. Be willing to change your diet if you experience heartburn or constipation/looseness. Your children's health can affect yours, from May onward (their flu becomes yours, etc.)

LIBRA

September 23 – October 22

Start nothing significant or important:
February 16 to March 9
June 18 to July 12
October 13 to November 3.

GENERAL:

Your career standing is solid through April, making these first four months a good time to look at your long-range career future, and to make decisions/plans for the decade ahead — including, if applicable, changing careers.

The opposite side of your life, home and family, needs care and caution (and, probably, a bit of repair) during the same first four months.

From May onward, your domestic sphere blossoms with good luck — the best in a decade!

May also begins 18 months which favour social rituals, big ideas, far travel and international affairs (import/export, for example) legal, intellectual, ethical, higher learning, publishing and love — deep, mature, (almost) unconditional love. But don't waste your time, May onward, on local travel, details and small ideas, chatter, errands and mere paperwork.

Your work continues (2011 to 2025) to demand sympathy and intuition (rather than hard logic and severity). Health-wise, viral complaints are in the forefront.

2020 is not a big year for romance (2021 will be!). But two very significant circumstances could wrap you up in the warm arms of partnership. Lust is a powerful force, now into 2026. Taurus draws you in mysterious ways. Gemini wants romance and marriage. And an Aries says, "Hey, what about me?" So there's not a lot of romance, but there are buckets full of sex, love and potential partnership.

LUCK:

"Luck" is always of two kinds: the normal, daily or monthly luck that Jupiter (optimism and great worldly luck) and Venus (sweet love, attractions, and mild but good luck). And "karma," the ongoing result of actions we took and patterns we started and wove in the past, that now is rewarding us, or wrapping us in the punishing, restricting web of our own actions/consequences.

Jupiter:

This lucky planet spends the entire year (except late December) in your sector of real estate, home and family. This is your best year in over a decade to find a place to put down roots, to buy or rent a new home. Your family will bubble with optimism and adventure. But read "Karma" below for important dates.

Venus:

This is your own ruling planet, and it governs love in general. For you, it also rules major finances, investment, health and lifestyle choices. Venus will bless you in early January (romance) February (partnership) March (sex and finances) and April to early August (law, love, travel, learning) August (career) September (light love, friends) October (with gov't or head office) November (your own charms radiate) and December (money and friends — travel at Xmas). Venus will make this one of your best years.

Karma:

Until May, your "good" karma lies in ambition, career, status, reputation, and prestige relations. Here, a calm, smooth and productive path awaits you.

If you want to fail during these first four months, bend your efforts toward home, real estate, security, Mother Nature, rest, sleep, diet/food, children, and business premises or territory. In these, you'll experience subtle but eventually solid disappointment.

From May onward (to January 2022) you'll find a smooth path in higher learning, international affairs, far travel, legal, intellectual, publishing and cultural involvements — and love. More than the usual number of single Librans will wed in 2020 and 2021.

If you want to fail in 2020, spend all your time in errands, gossip and chatter, news media, paperwork, filing systems, short trips — and keep your relationships casual.

LOVE:

Though no major planets support love for you this year, two minor planets do, and in a big way: Mars and Venus.

Mars rules partnerships and marriage for you, and it spends six months (July to year's end) in your marriage sign. It's almost certain that someone will chase you — this person is not shy. (Sometimes this is a love or hate, love or war influence — choose love!) From early September to mid-November, a lover's enthusiasm might wane briefly, or a powerful ex-mate might re-appear. A brand new suitor (if he/she shows September-November) might possess sexual problems.

Mars triggers casual friendships January/February…one of these might morph into a friendly love affair. April to mid-May, Mars sparks romantic intensity. This interval can bring a future mate, so be receptive! (If you're in an ongoing bond, April might nudge you toward co-habitation or marriage.)

Venus rules Libra (that is, you, your overall life) — and sex. This year (and a few to come) romance will probably arise suddenly, unexpectedly, and can swiftly plunge to another, deeper level. It will likely attract you to "thick" people — calm, slow, sensual and stubborn. This planet can trigger romance the first half of January (which develops probably through February). Venus sparks sex in March.

From April to August, Venus sits in one of your major love signs, Gemini. This can bring a life-changing love affair, one that dovetails with Mar's powerful partnership push, outlined above. Gemini is your sign of weddings, and every Gemini has a deep soft spot for Librans. All this can result in a life-mate, even a wedding ceremony. (If you're already living together, but have toyed with the idea of formal nuptials, you could not ask for a better time!) However, you might meet delays or indecision mid-May to late June. This is a good planning or assessing time involving love. Don't push these few weeks, let what comes, come. One who loves you might even delay into mid-July. That's okay. These delays are natural, so be patient. You won't be disappointed.

If you're married, April to August is a great time to take the family on an international journey, to expand their view of the world, and to teach them morals/ethics.

In September, Venus brings social joys and private optimism. Your charisma soars in October, which gives you the "commanding hand" in love. November attracts casual affairs — December too. (Late December starts a year of additional, swelling romance!)

Uranus, your romance planet, will do three things now to 2026: 1) tie romance closely to sexual intimacy; 2) might attract you to destruction — i.e., an extra-marital affair; and/or 3) can draw you toward Taurus people (especially April-born Taurus) even to the point of marriage.

If you're young and married, you might have a bit of difficulty becoming pregnant, now to 2026. If you experience this, enlist medical help. You might adopt, or embrace a step-child. (Remember, an adopted or step child's animosity, if it exists, covers fear.)

CAREER / BUSINESS:

Until May, your career sails along, protected from all "bumps." These are an excellent four months to change careers or employers, or to make good long-term decisions.

Co-workers "love you" the second half of January to early February. February holds work, and new instructions, but mid-month to March 9 brings indecision, misread instructions, delays and false starts. Be patient. July boosts your ambitions and career efforts, and August brings the rewards. (Even if only praise or a wink from the boss.) (But don't start any new practical projects the first 11 days of July.) Your social skills can help with a job or gov't-related efforts in September. Asking for a pay raise in October probably won't work, as indecision and uncertainty creeps in. Chase money in November (and December) instead.

Bosses are impatient, temperamental, late April to June 11 — be diplomatic and keep your sense of humour. Don't push higher-ups during this interval.

From May onward (into 2021) the benevolent "protection" that imbues your career will switch to more intellectual areas, including far travel, higher learning, law, publishing, etc. If your career leans this way, good! (E.g., lawyers and academics among you will prosper.)

Also from May onward, you might shoot forward more lucratively in real estate than in career. (I don't advise quitting your usual career, tho.) If you work in mining, forestry, agriculture, construction/demolition, child care and similar fields, May to December will expand your work and bring much good fortune.

From July to year's end, many opportunities (and possible partnerships) confront you. Be willing to leap, to commit. But take care September 9 to November 13, when the opportunities that arise might deflate later.

HOME / FAMILY:

2020 is a great year to rest and recuperate. Old fears and "ghosts" dissolve. You can throw skeletons out of the closet. Healing is available through family discussions. Your family will be buoyant, optimistic, ready for big home-based projects or vacation adventures. (Time to take the kids to visit another continent?)

This is your best year in over a decade to buy a new home or any kind of real estate. You'll probably find the best buys or most lovely home within a day's driving of your present home.

However, wait until May 6 onward (to mid-December) to act on anything home-related. Before May, this area holds good luck, but also bad karma — and karma's stronger, causing delays, dead ends, or "disappointment down the road." Perhaps the biggest danger is over-expansion or over-optimism. For instance, the banker tells you interest rates are so low you can afford 2 x the house you were looking at. So you buy a huge house, then in 2 years interest rates shoot upward, your mortgage payments triple, and you lose the house. That's expansion, before May.

From May 6 onward your luck in real estate and home is unimpeded, strong and "purely lucky." Wait until this period to act. Best time to buy (or sign a new lease): mid-September to mid-December. These months are good for realty (or furniture or other home-related) purchases: May, September and November.

It's a lovely year to bring a baby or two into the world. (Twins are a bit more likely than usual.) It's also a great time to raise and teach kids.

FINANCES / INVESTMENT / DEBT:

Your major finances (stocks, bonds, investments and major debt) face very interesting times from 2019 to 2026. You will be creative and inventive with finances and taxes. But you will also face unpredictable, sudden events — e.g., stock market swings. The advice is obvious: be patient, try to foresee events. On the plus side, you will be, overall, lucky.

Your best investment, May to December, lies in real estate or associated fields: construction, furniture, carpet, paint and dish manufacturers, diaper companies, children's clothes, food companies, agriculture, mines, forestry, etc. (Stay out of these areas before May.)

Before May, and generally to 2026, you can profit from investments in beauty, pleasure, casinos and vacation destinations (e.g., "Sandals") fashions, sports, gaming and toy companies — and films. If going into business for yourself, these are potentially profitable areas to be in. So is anything to do with sensual love, sex, art and design.

Some of your best financial inspirations come in late April, late August and early September, and late December. Don't invest from mid-May to July 11, unless it is an opportunity from the past that returns now.

Your earnings should be good in November and the first half of December.

HEALTH:

Note: I am not a doctor, so these comments are general, and do not necessarily apply to you.

Your health difficulties often centre on gastro-intestinal, kidney, liver, bladder and blood zones. Iron is often lacking, or too abundant. These vulnerabilities have reached a peak in 2018/19 and through April this year. From May onward these areas improve immensely. Still, make sure you have a healthy diet, for all these, even kidneys and blood, have their foundation in nutrition.

From 2009 to 2025, venereal diseases are possible, especially from casual sex. Keep condoms handy. Watch for rusty nails and other underfoot hazards, especially at home, same years. The period 2018 to 2026 presents an unusual health factor: your nervous system (or simple stress) can impact you. To cure stress, reduce television watching, and increase gardening, nature walks, outdoor exercise, meditation (maybe) and relaxation techniques. Romance can make you nervous when it gets very intimate very fast.

.

SCORPIO

October 23 – November 21

Start nothing significant or important:
February 16 to March 9
June 18 to July 12
October 13 to November 3.

GENERAL:

Your world is changing, 2019 to 2026. In 6 years you'll look back and think, "Wow, how far I've come." Most of the changes will come through relationships, and will affect your home. (For instance, your spouse could say, "We're moving to Africa.") Some of these changes will be sudden and unexpected. A Taurus person might be involved.

Many sparkling new relationships will pop up this year — good ones. (These new links come through short trips, errands, email, etc. — from your life's daily rounds.) Those that arise before May will not be quite as fortunate/compatible as those that come May onward.

A tremendous amount of work faces you from July to December.

A huge, lucrative financial streak visits you from April to August.

Relationships are unpredictable, but 2020 offers both many new contacts, and a long streak of satisfying physical intimacy. Be wary of extra-marital temptations.

Romance remains a potent force (2011-2025). If you're unattached, 2020 can bring true love — but 2022 will also.

Until May, your gift of gab might seduce the wrong person — in other words, you can talk yourself into a bit if a dead-end. Before May also, far travel, higher education, publishing and profound ideas bless you, but short trips and idle chatter "defeat you" (most probably by wasting your time).

From May to December, you will be wise, calm and correct when choosing investments or other financial actions. But, same period, don't do anything "extra" for $ — over-focusing on earnings will undermine your luck.

LUCK:

 "Luck" is always of two kinds: the normal, daily or monthly luck that Jupiter (optimism and great worldly luck) and Venus (sweet love, attractions, and mild but good luck). And "karma," the ongoing result of actions we took and patterns we started and wove in the past, that now is rewarding us, or wrapping us in the punishing, restricting web of our own actions/consequences.

Jupiter:

This lucky planet spends 11 and a half months in your sector of mail, communications, errands, office systems and paperwork, short trips, curiosity, local media and details. Until May, though, try to keep these activities to a minimum, because they might contain subtle traps, cause unexpected reactions (most of which will be hidden from you) and draw you into unprofitable relationships or projects. May onward, these activities will benefit you, perhaps immensely. They can connect you to a potential lover, mate, business partner, opportunities, relocation, negotiations and agreements.

Venus:

For you, Scorpio, Venus represents partnership, marriage, and opposition. (Usually, your opposition will be slightly hidden or subtle, and often can come from the other things Venus rules for you: gov't, head office or institutions.) Venus promotes love and opportunity for you mid-January to early February, March, August, October (light love) and late November to mid-December.

Karma:

Through April, Cancers give you the best advice; May to December, Geminis give you the best advice. Also through April, higher learning, foreign-born people, far travel, law and intellectual or cultural pursuits go well, with calm wisdom. But the short side of these, local travel, chatter, daily communications, errands and paperwork, details and local media cause wasted time, delays, and unsatisfying results. From May to December, investments, research, deep sex, debt reduction, medical procedures and lifestyle changes draw you down a smooth, productive and blessed path. Make a commitment (or 2 or 3) — the consequence will please you!

But, same period, don't chase daily/monthly earnings, nor buy depreciating assets (e.g., a car). Not a good time to demand a pay raise, nor to try making money by buying and selling. E.g.: if you own a retail store, sales aren't great (but your store's/business's value will likely rise, same time). Or, on the stock market, avoid high dividend payers; opt for stocks promising capital gains.

LOVE:

Love will lean heavily toward sexual desire and intimacy in 2020, Scorpio. From April to early August, your marriage planet will stay in your sex sign. If you're looking for love, listen to your physical desires — they will point to the right mate for you. Whatever happens, you will remember this year as one of the sexiest in your life. A Taurus, Gemini or Libra might be involved. (By the way, some people consider sex a "lower form" of love, or somehow "dirty." You know it's not. It's actually the most important, or humans would not exist. But even more, this year — and all 2021, also — sex itself is karmically blessed. If you could ask a little angel, "what should I do to improve my spiritual side?" the little angel would say, "Have sex." (Or more politely, "procreate.")

Earlier, January gives hints of attraction, but doesn't lead to much. March brings someone who embodies both romance and partnership. But until March 9, he or she should be a returnee from the past — brand new potential amours won't work unless you meet after March 9. You might exchange love's whispers right into mid-April.

Late April and May contain exciting meetings with someone who has the markings of a great partner — but domestic strife or rumblings at work might interfere, or add stress to an already "excitable" or tense relationship/situation.

June's in the middle of that April-August "lust fest." It deepens the desire, and perhaps any secrecy surrounding it. But mid-May to late June also slows the love wagon — unavoidable circumstances might temporarily separate you from your squeeze. Or indecision emerges, as you wonder if mere sex is enough to base a lifetime on. Romance is dynamic rather than harmonious. At the same time, your romantic courage is super-high, and you're determined to express yourself, to press your ardor. Complicated! But love will win out. You might hook up with a co-worker May/June.

July is a natural wedding month, and a time of gentle, broad-based, mental sweetness — the kind of amour in which the head melts before the heart, but before long everything melts, heart and soul! August continues this to some degree, and the answer will likely be Yes to a proposal. But you face a tremendous amount of work July/August also, which can interfere with the course of love. September brings friends, popularity, but continues that hard work — it does not fight your love life, but it might weary you a bit. ("Not now, Honey, I'm tired.")

October echoes September's friendly gatherings, but you're tired, your charisma is low, and by mid-month (to November 2) you fall into indecision, which causes delays and "incompletions." (If you don't feel indecisive, delays will come from outside, perhaps from your lover.) In November, your charisma surges, and by mid-month you express yourself in persuasive ways, especially in intimate clinches.

December offers casual sex, with a person who might bore you in time. Think before embracing.

CAREER / BUSINESS:

You will work yourself to your limits from July to year's end. My advice: split your days in two: half for work, half for love. Neither should be the only thing. To do this, you might have to establish a hard-and-fast schedule for work, say 40 hours a week, and let love have the rest.

> Whether you're in management or on the shop floor, the last half of 2020 emphasizes hands-on work. It isn't so much that hands-on is lucky or favourable; it's inevitable. So roll up your sleeves and get busy. (Management or delegating tasks will succeed January through April — and I advise avoiding hand's-on during these 4 months. Why? Because it gives others an opening to rise above you, or order you. Managing, instead, lets you control the workplace situation — and your place in it. But be realistic.) You will make the most progress July to early September, and mid-November through December. The period in-between might bring job roles from the

past, indecision, or re-planning.

January involves you in paperwork and communications. You might need to travel for your job. Co-workers are very pleasant in February — you might be asked to work creatively, or to lead a "social" work event. In March, your tasks involve errands, short trips, paperwork and swift, easy chores. A light, unimportant time until late March. Then, into April through mid-May, one job might end and another begin. If you have contemplated quitting this year, April/May is the time.

In June, your job might involve research or financial actions — research is a lot safer, and more fortunate. If advising your boss(es) tell them to wait until mid-July before pulling the trigger on a big outlay, purchase of big equipment or buying out another company, etc. Romance is powerful this May/June — don't let it interfere with your job. You can really impress higher-ups with your creative abilities.

June/July are intellectual, promote far travel, legal and media ventures, but delays and false starts in this area counsel waiting until July 11 to begin anything new. Now your work begins to intensify.

Late July/August highlight your career progress and ambitions. Prestige relations and worldly standing are in focus. You'll do well! September isn't as strong in this elevated zone, but still aids your ambitions and nudges higher-ups to favour you and your projects.

In October, conserve your strength. You might have to deal with gov't, head office or institutions, perhaps to obtain permission or specialized information. Indecision slows forward progress mid-October to November 2. December doesn't stop the huge work effort demanded of you — but it might bring part of the first reward for all your endeavours, in money form!

Creative workers (writers, artists, actors, inventors, designers, etc.) will have a good 2020 — in fact, in general, a good 2011-to-2025. What I've written above about work times, influences, etc., still apply to you, but with less weight, less intensity.

HOME / FAMILY:

Early January gives your home a boost, promotes family affection. Late month and February increase the domestic atmosphere. Normally this would be a good time to renovate, repair or decorate, landscape, even find a new home, but not this year, as delays, misinformation and false starts affect you from mid-February to early March. Still, February/March is a great time to raise and teach children. If you have no firm goals in this late winter period, you'll be happy, basking in the glow of family affection and fun.

April/May bring domestic strife, so walk softly. Physical work on the home will replace or soften conflict.

2020 is kind of a "window year," as it introduces a sobriety and realism into your domestic zone from late March through June, and again the last half of December.

In 2020 this is slight and thin (as an influence) but it shows what will exist in 2021, 22 and 23: work, practicality, duties and patience will characterize your domestic sphere. From late December 2020 through December '21, you face one of the best home-buying periods in 30 years. (Read the "Investments" section below for more clues.) In 2020 you might have to grapple with someone's disabilities at home. (Especially if you recently married a Gemini.) No worries — this is a loving thing.

June is potentially a month of changes, but this year indecision reigns, so little major change will result. (Save big home changes for next year, when they'll be very fortunate.) In August, be willing to abandon the domestic scene for awhile, to focus on your outside interests, including career. September's a good time for a garden or dinner party. Socialize, have friends over a few times — October, too, although your energy isn't high this month. A good time to snuggle at home, rest, sleep. November/December are probably better spent at work, earning money, than at home.

FINANCES / INVESTMENT / DEBT:

2020 and 2021 are probably the best and wisest financial/investment years in the 18 years past, and the 18 ahead. 2020 is lucky in "pure investment," especially from April to early August. 2021 will be very fortunate in real estate investments. (Or debt reduction — e.g., pay down the mortgage.)

All year, money luck or earnings are tied to messaging, travel, visits, communications, paperwork and swift, easy chores. This luck is unreliable, perhaps even negative before May, and beneficial, even hugely so, from May to December. For instance, communicating with another employer, or sending him/her an application, could lead to a boost in earnings. (March "quickens" this influence, but holds dangers from impulsiveness — don't send unedited text [i.e., read before sending] or shoot off at the mouth, even in a buoyant, nice way.)

Extra money flows toward you January to mid-February. Bank this, avoid debt and over-spending, or you could end with less. You have an almost unconscious desire, now, to spend. You might spend on your home in February, but don't launch any big projects, renovations, etc., because mid-month starts a few weeks of mistakes, false starts, etc.

April brings work, and pay. And perhaps an unexpected agreement or temporary partnership. This month also starts a very favourable investment climate for you, stretching right into early August. My advice: invest or manipulate your finances April to mid-May, then study them mid-May to June 25, then invest again until August. You could take home the prize! (Finances can be up and down, a bit erratic during the mid-May through June period. Not a good time to gamble. You might win, but can you take a loss?)

A tremendously long intense work period starts in July, and lasts through year's end — you'll be paid, of course, and might work overtime. If all this work proves you're indispensable, then ask for a pay raise. July might bring you to invest in international, legal, publishing/media, academic or cultural venues. August is similar, but this month you might be dealing with the "big boys." In September, these "big boys" (or simply your bosses) will do you a favour — ask for it.

Use August to December earnings to pay down debt. If you're debt free, bank your earnings for 2021, when a splendid real estate purchase will await you. (Pay down debt so your mortgage qualifications will rise for next year.)

Gov't-related investments (or anything heavily regulated, such as utility companies) can do well in October and November — but take no financial action October 13 to November 3.

In December, look forward: December 20 starts 12 months of great good luck in the home — and in real estate or any home-related zones. This period will also bring sobriety and practicality, realism and patience to any home-related project. There's no rush. For many Scorpios, a home bought in 2021 will form a foundation that grows in health and wealth for many years — decades.

HEALTH:

Note: I am not a doctor, so these comments are general, and do not necessarily apply to you.

It's not usually your weak spot, Scorpio, but 2019 to 2026 increases your stress levels, especially in relationships and when you are chasing opportunities. The best cure: be mellow in relationships, refuse to let others bother or bait you. (This stress can also come from good, positive love attractions.)

Take care of your feet, ankles and wrists. From July through December, guard against sudden temperature changes, rashes, itching, arthritis, cuts, burns and headaches or blows to the head. If something starts here in, say, July or September, it won't go away quickly — so get aid, salve, etc. Over-the-counter cures will tend to be sufficient, as these are mostly minor irritations.

On a deep crucial level, your health will actually be better than it has been for a long time!

SAGITTARIUS

November 22 – December 21

Start nothing significant or important:
February 16 to March 9
June 18 to July 12
October 13 to November 3.

GENERAL:

Relationships glow with love and significance this year. It's odd, because the major planets hint that 2020 should be a relatively loveless yet excellent earnings and money year. But Venus and Mars, the two romantic planets, have other intentions. They intend to make 2020 one of your most powerful romantic and marriage years in at least a quarter century. Venus, the planet of love, grace, marriage and affection, spends over four months in your marriage/partnership house. Mars, your planet of romance, is not about to be ignored — it spends over six months in your sign of romance. If you're single, this is a banner year!

2020 should be a splendid, lucky income year. However, before May, earnings might disappoint — or, you might chase an earnings situation (or a purchase, say of a car) that promises the sky, but delivers only the muddy puddle it was reflected in. From May to December, earnings and purchases hit a lucky streak: keep you eyes open for major bargains!

As it has for some years — and will until 2025 — your home is a deep, true, real home, but you might be a little lazy here, or a "late sleeper."

Work and health face change from 2019 to 2026. You'll deal with unexpected conditions. Workmates will be friendly and unpredictable. Communications and travel become major forces in your employment. Saturn has dampened your income for several years, and will in 2020 — but the walls of denial are cracking: this Spring lets you "escape" these earnings restrictions, and December ends them forever (well, for 3 decades ahead).

Before May, investments and finances, and owning your own business, are favoured, whereas earnings are not. May to December, karma warns you against ultra-independence, and promises smooth, satisfying results where you co-operate, join forces, and are inter-dependent. (This applies in love, too.)

LUCK:

"Luck" is always of two kinds: the normal, daily or monthly luck that Jupiter (optimism and great worldly luck) and Venus (sweet love, attractions, and mild but good luck). And "karma," the ongoing result of actions we took and patterns we started and wove in the past, that now is rewarding us, or wrapping us in the punishing, restricting web of our own actions/consequences.

Jupiter:

This planet of luck is your sign's ruler. In 2020, it brings luck in earnings, purchases, casual sex (not recommended in this powerful love year) memory and rote learning. Your income is certain to increase. But read "Karma" below for timing.

Venus:

Venus blesses you, April to August, in love, marriage, partnership, relocation, opportunities, negotiations and contracts. These might hit a lull or indecision's delay mid-May to late June. Venus sweetens your home with affection January/February, sparks romance February, and makes work and co-workers more affectionate in March, promotes sex in August and bright thoughts, gentle love in September. In October, this planet nudges higher-ups to favour you. In November she brings friends; in December, peace.

Karma:

Before May, your money motives might not be the best; as a result, your income ventures could actually backfire. After May, your income luck soars — more will come in than most years. A pay raise is almost certain — ask for it! Before May, seek advice from Cancer (and those whose first name starts with M or O); ignore advice from Capricorns (and those whole first initial is S, H or Y). Chase big finances, investments, but avoid wasteful purchases, and focusing strongly on earnings. May to December, seek advice from Gemini (and those whose first name begins with E, X or a sibilant C — e.g., "Cindy," not "Cathy"). But reject advice from Sagittarius (and those whose first name starts with J or U). May onward, reject independence — be a joiner, realize others might (this year, not usually!) have a better world and ethical view than you.

LOVE:

Venus, the planet of love, grace, marriage and affection, spends over four months in your marriage/partnership sign (April to early August). In ordinary years, Venus spends only one month here.

Mars (your romantic planet) is not to be outdone. It spends over six months from July to early 2021 in your sign of romance. In most years, Mars spends only six weeks in this area.

If you're single, this is a banner year! This combination of both Venus and Mars spending four times their usual sojourn in any sign is rare; for them both to spend these intervals in your love signs, is very rare. (I'm not looking, but I would guess this occurs maybe once a century.)

If you're already married, Venus will bring sweet harmony to your marriage, April to August. If you're single, the result is obvious: you could form a bond that is affectionate and strong, one that, even if it doesn't last (and it should) will be something you remember all your life. One potential flaw: you might be attracted to two people, which causes confusion, delay and love's indecision in May/June.

Mars, not to be outdone, cranks up your romantic courage, July to year's end. Your temper will shout a lot, but your passion for someone glows hot for six months. Same period, be gentle with children — you might push them too aggressively.

True love is a definite possibility. A Gemini and/or an Aries figure prominently — so might a Leo.

Generally, January to April encourages or gives a cosmic blessing to, sex and boudoir intimacy of a deep, serious kind. (Good time to seek pregnancy.) As odd as it sounds, an extra-marital affair might actually bless and improve your life and outlook, whereas usually such shenanigans would hurt everyone emotionally.

January is sensual, promotes easy, casual intimacy — but with someone who will probably bore you, long-term. (This is an "option" all year, but I would reject it, as real, true, knock-your-socks-off romance awaits you later in 2020.) Still, you are filled with romantic courage and impatience January through mid-February, like a racehorse straining to start. (February can bring a friendly romance — one that could lead to a light, fairly casual marriage.) March again offers that casual sex, the one without much heart.

April is always your love month. This one will be replete with sudden meetings, exciting calls, and friendly, maybe eccentric suitors. Now serious love might begin. You will start to see the value, the potential happiness, in a relationship with a peer. The one you will marry or live with might enter now, or anytime to August. If you're already attached, April begins a "love-fest" that won't end before 2021. (Okay, maybe "months of affection.") April through June takes away your gift of gab; communications become a little slower: so form your words carefully and slowly in love situations.

May is for work, but June lights up the love machine again. Two suitors might exist, or something about the one you're attracted to gives you pause — or he/she is simply out of town for work, etc. In any case, indecision and delay affect a prime bond. Be patient and gracious; delays will end and love will be even stronger mid-July into August. If someone asks you to marry April to August, consider saying "Yes!"

August is for weddings. A foreign-born person might attract you, or a foreign-country honeymoon. If you're still seeking someone, travel afar, or attend school, visit law courts, libraries or transportation hubs.

September's ambitious, but still retains that "wedding" (and travel) influence. This month to mid-November might slow down the passion train temporarily, or bring a hot old flame, or might briefly cause sexual obstacles/flagging. If you meet someone new and start a love affair during these 9 weeks, he (yourself if you're the male) sexual problems might exist permanently. (If you're the female, you might grow critical and attack his ego during this period — don't, of course!)

December is made for love, and might be the climax of the year! Romance soars, your charisma draws others — if you haven't yet, make the leap into love's seas now.

CAREER / BUSINESS:

This is a good income year, probably bringing you a boost in earnings. However, it isn't the best career phase. You might climb ambition's ladder a bit, especially from late August to late October.

If you're in business for yourself, January to April buoys your efforts and assets — but not necessarily your income. (A tempting scheme to boost earnings might be a fiasco, so examine it — and your motives — carefully. Look ahead, try to spot potential snags.)

May onward, your income will soar.

Work earnings are favoured in early January. Avoid launching new career/business-related ventures mid-February to March 9. (Instead, protect ongoing projects from delays and supply shortages — preferably before they occur.) But your executive abilities surge upward mid-February through March, while others drown in indecision — advantage: you.

Co-workers are friendly in March. Money can rush toward you January/February — bank it, don't spend.

Pressures ease in April, as love crowds out work. Work goes well the first half of May, then "discussions" take over. Many opportunities late May/June. But work hits a reef of confusion, delays and mistakes mid-June to July 11.

In August/September, your work might take you to foreign shores, to school or to lawyers. (All's well.) In October, work mates want to socialize — good, jump in. Bosses, parents and VIPs favour you this month. Don't start brand new ventures, mid-October to November 2. The gov't might contact you about a neglected task/taxes, or an application you made previously. Take a management approach in November — delegate tasks. December's for fun, not work! (But if you want to throw your weight around or be a leader in the workplace, December's the time.)

HOME / FAMILY:

From 2011 to 2025, your planet of home (Neptune) crawls through your sign of home and domesticity. This happens every 165 years. Both worry and sleep reign in 2020's home. Avoid drugs/alcohol at home. January to April is not a good time to change homes or buy a new home. From May to December, buying is "okay." (Your best home-buying times will be mid-May through July next year (2021) and January to early May 2022.)

As with most years from 2011-25, water is a force to be reckoned with. Check the plumbing and groundwater tables before buying or renting.

Your ruling planet, lucky Jupiter, will spend all the present year, 2020, in a good, productive, mildly fortunate aspect to your home sector. So no major drama or catastrophe will occur — instead, this is a good year to tinker and repair, paint and decorate. Your garden will be a pleasure. The children will be — as kids go — relatively well-behaved and enjoy normal or better growth in learning. Your youngsters will be very optimistic, very hopeful, and social — they'll bring more friends around.

Your home is a sweet, affectionate refuge the last half of January and early February. It's a good time for home gatherings, encouraging the kids, decoration and painting, and planting flower bulbs.

You'll be indecisive about your home, property and family the last half of February into March 9. NOT a good time to renovate, decorate, landscape, or build.

From April to August, you face tremendous good luck in relationships. If you're married, this nudges you and your spouse to work happily together on domestic chores, or to let the chores go and just be loving. If you're single and a parent, your kid(s) might not accept someone new at first, but they'll soon see this "intruder" as someone sweet and reliable — and someone who offers them, security. He/she will be accepted! If you're single and facing co-habitation, these few months might present a dilemma: you and your love might not agree on the right or "perfect" home. A compromise or two might be wise on your part, since you'll still get most of what you want.

From mid-May to late June your temper runs hot at home. Taking care of neglected chores or repairs (or going to the gym) will use up your energy and reduce your feistiness. (Don't start large renovations as it will be difficult to pick colours, textures, designs, etc. that will please you later. In addition, the second half of June brings almost a month of mistakes, indecision and "missing workmen."

You will be filled with passion, creative and inventive energy from July to year's end. Don't let yourself push children too hard during these six months. That creative burst could result in major decorations, but avoid these the first half of July and mid-October to early November.

All in all, a good home year!

FINANCES / INVESTMENT / DEBT:

The last couple of years have been difficult for your income, although 2019 favoured investments (but probably dragged your earnings down a bit, or increased your expenses). That weight is lifted now, partly by May onward, partly by December. You might also notice that income restrictions — what I call a "weight" — lift a bit from April through June. This period is a hint of the future, of freedom in money affairs, to start in 2021.

Overall, 2020 "repays" you for all the money difficulties of the past two years. Your income will expand strongly, your bank account will swell! But take care in pursuing income or other money schemes before May — a trap might lurk. Instead of chasing immediate money, put your energy into investments, or buy/start a business.

From May onward, incoming dollars should rise and rise. Put extra income in investments, or pay down debt. From July to year's end, romance, creative projects or the hunt for beauty or pleasure, can "fight" both your income and your investments or net worth. (Put another way, chasing money, or holding it selfishly, can interfere with romance, et al. So in a way it's your choice — love or money.)

July is your best investment month — but wait until July 12 onward to pull the trigger.

HEALTH:

Note: I am not a doctor, so these comments are general, and do not necessarily apply to you.

Your usual area of health problems are your hips and thighs. (For example, back ache might occur because your hips are out of kilter — ask your doctor about this.)

In crucial health matters, you get a free ride until May. That month might bring a bit of stress, but more importantly it cautions you to be careful with electricity and sharp tools/machines. At times your stomach might feel light (or as if your last meal is "floating"). Be vigilant in making sure food is fresh, and that water seepage, mold or other "moist" conditions are kept away.

CAPRICORN

December 22 – January 19

Start nothing significant or important:
February 16 to March 9
June 18 to July 12
October 13 to November 3.

GENERAL:

Great good fortune wraps you in its cheerful arms all 2020, Cap! What a change from last year! Still, two things to note: 1) before May, the clouds of 2019 still hang over you, although they're dissipating; and 2) for you, great good luck always comes with a responsibility attached. For instance, you get a pay raise, but have to supervise more people/projects. (You don't mind this extra burden — in fact, you almost seek it, for as your responsibilities increase, so does your sense of self-worth.)

Your income will be affected by sober conditions, and might cause a lowering of earnings (or, same thing, an increase in expenses) in the Spring. Be fiscally conservative.

Relationships bless you January to April. Be willing to join, to abandon what might be an untenable position. Others — especially your business partner, spouse, the public reaction at large — will be your best moral guides.

From May to December, lean toward hands-on work, and away from managing/delegating. Your interactions with head office or gov't agencies will be tricky, frustrating, so avoid bureaucrats as much as possible.

Romance, from 2018 to 2026, will be unpredictable, exciting, perhaps tension-inducing, and oddly friendly. In 2020, love can blossom with a co-worker (or someone in your field).

Your casual, everyday contacts connect you with psychic, intuitive people. You remain somewhat indecisive and passive about chatting, calling, emails and texts. (This influence covers 2011 to 2025.) But you can communicate with others in a healing, sympathetic and empathic way.

You might build something very solid, remarkable and lasting, especially if you start in October to mid-December. (But this "big thing" will be on your mind as a possibility all year.) Could be a business, a structure, a reputation — whatever. It's practical and prosperous.

LUCK:

"Luck" is always of two kinds: the normal, daily or monthly luck that Jupiter (optimism and great worldly luck) and Venus (sweet love, attractions, and mild but good luck). And "karma," the ongoing result of actions we took and patterns we started and wove in the past, that now is rewarding us, or wrapping us in the punishing, restricting web of our own actions/consequences.

Jupiter:

This planet stays in your sign all year, except the last two weeks of December. It will bring you optimism, friendly cheerfulness and rising popularity (because people like friendly people). It also brings tremendous luck — sometimes all year. Sometimes Jupiter stays "silent" for months, then suddenly releases a bountiful bombshell. Your luck will be highest (but unreliable, perhaps even "false") before mid-May, and mid-September onward (without any "qualifications" — just pure luck). Hard to explain what this good luck affects, because it exists in your "personality" sign of Capricorn — basically, it affects YOU. But it does carry hints of management, delegation, secrets, institutions and gov't —an area of temptation and false promise in 2020 — so even luck, this year, needs careful handling.

Venus:

For you, Venus rules romance and career/reputation. This planet brings you luck in January (your charms glow — good hair days). In February, Venus brings money luck — good time to buy a luxury item, nice clothes, jewelry, car, etc. In March, Venus spurs affection in communications, and in April, promotes a happy home and charming kids. April to August, this planet creates affection in the workplace, and could ignite a co-worker affair. In September, she helps you make the right investments. October, this planet brings lucky travel or school openings. November, Venus nudges higher-ups to favour you. Late month into December, this planet brings affectionate friends.

Karma:

From January through April, Cap, your "good karma" lies in relationships, far horizons, opportunities and co-operation. If you insist on acting independently, you might fail.

From May onward (right into early 2022) karma will subtly undercut/entrap you if you withdraw, focus on gov't, institutions or "head office." To ensure failure, work with agents, advisors, civil servants, spiritualists and charities.

To walk a smooth, productive and wise path, May to 2022, roll up your sleeves and get the job done yourself. Over-the-counter medicines serve you well. A great time to improve your nutrition.

LOVE:

From 2019 to 2026, your most intense romantic feelings will be sparked by someone eccentric, friendly, nerdy, intelligent, aware, a bit of a rebel, and unpredictable — a free spirit or an "electric personality."

If you're a parent, your children will act a bit like this — these years, they're touched by genius, but they might need some calming process (e.g., sports, hikes) as they're more nervous, high strung than usual. (Any child born in May, 2020-26, will be strongly determined, intelligent, and very, very social.)

Romance might be tied to money. "Casual love" prospects will judge you by your economic position (or dress). You'll be more possessive — even of a casual date. You will tend to chase people you feel friendly toward, and will find that sex comes quite easily, but doesn't have a "deep meaning." On the other hand, you might fall for someone who not only ignores money, but tries to live a life without it.

Weird, but this person would be the most thrilling one you'll meet in 2020. Love might be an odd combination of greed and selflessness. Hard to describe.

Romance is most likely to spark in early January, all March, late April, early July (an old flame, but in a new guise) late August into September, late October and late December.

A co-worker love affair is not certain, but quite possible, especially April to August.

Someone you meet January to April can capture your heart simply because he/she is good, moral — and would be a good advisor to you. May onward, love isn't denied, but this "cosmic goodness" leaves it.

If you're a male, be careful with sexual assertiveness January to mid-February. You'll be determined and brave, a "warrior," mid-February through March — this can attract female attention. (March is very romantic, but mildly indecisive — you might meet the right one in a gathering you attend.)

Whatever your sex, April into May can spark an intimate affair with someone who yields/agrees easily to sex, but will bore you eventually. September/October offer real romance, but sexual obstacles might occur. (If you're a man, January/February next year, 2021, will be very sexually potent, and very romantic.)

CAREER / BUSINESS:

Status is very important to you. 2020 does not hold a rocket to the top. But it does contain a four-plus month streak of luck and favour in your work, April to August — this will translate into brownie points with higher-ups, and prepares you for upward motion.

In addition, you are personally lucky in 2020, cheerful, outgoing and confident. This helps you storm the walls of power, or at least find an open door and walk in! Also, this personal uptick in luck seems to be tied to an increase in responsibilities, which itself is a step up the career stairway.

However, from May to December, don't seek progress in the halls of gov't, administration offices, in the political structure of institutions. Here, progress will be slow, or worse. You might not believe this, and actually can be tempted to enter this zone, as it promises easy rewards. But you will find these rewards elusive — like the donkey pursuing the dangling carrot. If your plans include a dive into bureaucracy, do this January through April. For example, if you need to apply for gov't permission to log that section, or to build a house or obtain a business license — anything — do it as early in 2020 as possible. (I.e., January.) With humility.

In general this year (and next) you will find real success AFTER April if you roll up your sleeves and tackle the work yourself, and a path studded with little frustrations if you insist on managing and delegating. Especially from April to August, unexpected rewards can accrue from your "I'll do it" attitude. Of course, you might already be in an advanced management roll. If so, from May to December "get out in the field" as much as possible, connect directly with employees, visit sites, personally peruse projects, files, cases, etc.

April and early May and late June to early August are a great time to either seek employment or hire new employees.

HOME / FAMILY:

2020's domestic developments are important and significant. From July to year's end, Mars will prompt you to develop, repair, renovate or otherwise tackle your abode with "warrior intensity." During these six months, you might be a little overbearing or impatient with children — keep it light!

Any arguments with your spouse will diminish if you get physically working on domestic tasks and projects.

2020 is a dicey time to buy real estate. But it's great for demolition, construction and renovations. You might sell a property (or home) to end a situation.

January to mid-February is a good time to work on your abode, or to find help for a child with disabilities or other problems. You can access gov't aid, such as utility or renovation grants, or programs for the disabled.

Mid-February through March, you can be tempted to end a situation — or, conversely, to work hard on a domestic or property project. But be careful — indecision and confusion, false starts and mistakes will rule before mid-March. This counsels sticking with whatever was started previously, rather than launch new projects.

April again features your home — and hefty spending on it, April and the first half of May. Start nothing mid-June to mid-July. August brings sweet affection with your spouse. September's mellow yet sexy. If you're young, it's a good month to seek pregnancy.

Overall, from 2018 to 2026, your children will display unique talents and unusual or very forward-looking opinions. You are likely to spend much more on your children than usual during these years, perhaps as a result of their talents (e.g., dance school). However, don't expect your kids to be predictable nor little princes or princesses; for 6 years to come, they will be very social, a bit rebellious, stubborn and kind, cool yet gentle. If a child is born this year, from July to year's end, he or she will be a warrior — assertive, a ball of fire in some aspect.

FINANCES / INVESTMENT / DEBT:

Your income will be affected by sober conditions, and might cause a lowering of earnings (or, same thing, an increase in expenses) in the Spring. An increase in expenses is more likely, as a lengthy, bountiful and fortunate streak of work-related earnings occurs this Spring and Summer. You should see your bank account swell April to early August — just in time for your best month — August — to pour extra funds into either paying down debt or increasing your investment holdings.

This is a harbinger of 2021 and 22, when income will be a serious focus. During these periods, be fiscally conservative. On the plus side, the heavenly body causing this "sober income" influence is your ruling planet, Saturn. This will nudge you into extra money efforts, and could even cause you to grow your income in solid — and big — ways.

So it's largely up to you.

On the investment side, no overwhelming influences exist, pro or con. (This in itself is rather good news, for it means you have an open field, that your choices matter more than "destiny.") However, you might be wise to avoid a long-term investment in high-tech, especially internet-related tech, electronics, social housing and "disruptive" industries or companies. These can be good for buying/selling — trading. But if you're holding such stocks or inventories, keep a cautious weather-eye on them. A good investment might be in dividend-yielding instruments in vacation, theme park, cruise or other "fun time" areas, as well as social sectors, such as dance or night clubs, introduction agencies or romantic gift manufactures/retailers.

Your best investment times are the first half of February (for income-yielding holdings) April to late July (machinery, tools, manufacturers/factories, mail and communications firms [e.g., DHS or Purolator] and anything to do with prosthetics) August (best month of all) September (luxury items — jewelry, etc.) and November (the "fun time" stocks mentioned above). (This list is not exhaustive, of course.)

You might also invest, almost any time this year, in income-producing situations, "cash cows" or start a business that depends on cash flow — e.g., a store. The reason is simple: 2021 will be a year of large earnings, so an early (i.e., 2020) preparation or set-up would be wise.

HEALTH:

Note: I am not a doctor, so these comments are general, and do not necessarily apply to you.

Your health looks almost as good as it can be, Cap, at least in major things. If minor physical illness does arise, it can usually be cured with over-the-counter medicines. This is a good year to stay out of the hospital, and away from spas and retreats. This last six months, July to December, might bring heartburn or other digestive disorders — I could be wrong, but they don't seem too serious. Watch for tension around money matters, and sudden, unexpected reactions in sex, particularly around late January into February, and late July into August.

AQUARIUS

January 20 – February 18

Start nothing significant or important:
February 16 to March 9
June 18 to July 12
October 13 to November 3.

GENERAL:

2020 is part of a long-term, burgeoning change in your home. You will be there, deeply involved and affected — in fact, you're the main instigator or architect of these changes. You will also grow more home-loving, more willing to skip that trip to Vegas to bask in the security of a comfy home. This might, at times, cause some friction with a more adventurous or restless spouse.

Until May, you'll find good, easy results from hands-on work. Same period, management types, civil servants and bureaucrats generally will dig in their heels and refuse to help — even, perhaps, in your case, to do their job. Avoid this area — and institutions, agents and advisors. Delegating tasks is asking for undone tasks.

May to year's end, you'll find joy and success in deep, passionate romance and creative projects, beauty and immediate indulgence in pleasure. Despite being, perhaps, madly in love, you will act calmly and wisely. But you'll court failure if you chase parties, group joys, social or political gatherings, flirtations and light, friendly romance. Not a good time for "committee creativity" nor for delaying pleasure to a future time. A group might even draw you into skullduggery or unscrupulous behaviour.

Speaking of romance, you'll find it this year!

Your income continues to be affected by Neptune, 2011 to 2025. You'll earn more if you listen to your hunches and intuition. Spend a wee bit on psychics or more establishment-approved consultants — they have good $ advice for you. (But in general avoid advisors/counsellors January through April.)

This year, the planet Saturn sticks a toe in the waters of your life. In 2021, Saturn will fully enter Aquarius, for two + years. So 2020 contains a hint of a growing skepticism, sobriety, maturity and seriousness of purpose that will pervade your 2021-22 future.

Your career and worldly ambitions have tried to shunt you into background areas since 2009 — gov't, administration, management and delegation, warehousing, institutions — and negatively, secrecy, drugs or other crime. This has had generally good, fruitful results. But this "background" zone has been negatively impacted for the last 14 months. That negative influence lasts through April this year, then disappears.

Intellectually, this is a "free" year — chase ideas, far travel, higher learning, weddings and other rituals, beliefs at will, especially this Autumn. Nothing makes you enter this zone, and nothing prevents you.

Local travel, conversations, paperwork and dealing with casual contacts will burn with intensity from July to year's end. You might buy a car — but don't drive like a maniac (you'll be tempted to!).

LUCK:

"Luck" is always of two kinds: the normal, daily or monthly luck that Jupiter (optimism and great worldly luck) and Venus (sweet love, attractions, and mild but good luck). And "karma," the ongoing result of actions we took and patterns we started and wove in the past, that now is rewarding us, or wrapping us in the punishing, restricting web of our own actions/consequences.

Jupiter:

This lucky planet spends all 2020 (except the last half of December) in your "background" sector of gov't, institutions, had office, spas and resorts, nursing, rest and recuperation, management and delegation of tasks. Usually, this brings luck to these areas — but it also "drains the luck" from other, perhaps more exciting zones. This is not a good year to challenge, compete, or seek public or social attention. (Read "Karma" below for qualifications about this background area.)

The best news: in late December Jupiter enters your own sign, Aquarius, and kicks off a whole year (2021) of the best luck in over a decade! Be patient for now.

Venus:

This planet rules love, luxury, and mild good luck for everyone. For you, it also rules home/family and intellect, profound ideas, far travel, higher learning, publishing/media, insurance, and law and rituals (e.g., weddings, bat mitzvahs, etc.). (She promotes these things — far travel, etc., in November.) Venus brings superb luck in romance, creative and pleasure pursuits — and in raising children — from April to early August. She helps you make more money (and purchase luxury items) in January, and makes your family more affectionate in March. In September, she sweetens relations with others, especially your spouse or business partners. In October,

Venus adds a fortunate edge to investments, and/or promotes sensual intimacy. In November/December, this planet helps you ascend ambitiously.

Karma:

From January to April, Aquarius, "karma" offers a smooth, productive and mellow path forward in hands-on work, daily health, machinery, and supporting dependents. If you want a rough ride, unfulfilled promises, and temptations to pervert your ethics/morals, then dig into gov't and institutional zones, deal with policy rather than accomplishment, manage and delegate.

From May to December (and on into 2021) to succeed, be "full hearted" — dive into romance, creative and speculative ventures, chase beauty and pleasure. If instead you want to fail, to hit dead-ends and untenable situations, stick with the crowd — seek popularity, social joys, attend/join groups, and opt for friendly, light romance.

LOVE:

Ah, sweet romance! Singles among you face a banner year (Spring, Summer) of amour, while married couples will rejoice in their children and each other.

You might make contact with someone who attracts you the second half of January. Your gift of gab lures someone. You attract others in February, when your energy and charisma shine. Affection might arise with a casual friend — this can become more serious, maybe very serious, from July into early 2021.

Mid-February to mid-April, it's more likely that a former money-related opportunity comes to you than a former lover, but the latter can occur. Remember, though, that this person bored you once, and will again — is a bit of boudoir embrace worth it? (Don't start any brand-new relationships before mid-March.) This "easy intimacy, eventual boredom" influence lasts into mid-April.

April through early August offers a stunning experience: someone appears who starts a love song singing in your heart. This is serious, Aquarius. A romance started now can at the least give an unforgettable four-month affair; at most, it might sculpt your life in

beauty and joy, bringing a life-long bond with true love. A Gemini might figure prominently. (So might a Virgo, but an affair with this sign will turn primarily sexual, and have many [perhaps minor] frictions.)

In May/June you might grow indecisive about love, or have two suitors to choose from, or your romantic partner might "go missing" for awhile — some delay will slow the love train. But all's well: by late June to August, romance resumes. Perhaps I'm exaggerating, but I think this could be a very significant bond. By August/September, you might marry or begin living together.

If you're a parent, April-to-August enhances your children's charms and talents. (Even earlier, in March, your heart swells with love for your children — and, if you have no kids, for the earth, or your home). It's an excellent time to begin home schooling, or to build a tree fort or a stage for them to act upon. If your kids are older, hmm, not sure. They will probably be out chasing young romance. But it's a good time to enroll them in fine arts or performance classes, to teach them a foreign language, etc.

If you're trying to become pregnant, September/October bless you. Someone talks marriage in October/November.

Friends join you in celebration (and perhaps a flirtation) in December, but don't expect much from this. (If you want to know why, read "Luck-Karma" (above).

CAREER / BUSINESS:

No planet occupies your career and ambition sector for most of 2020. This gives you a free hand to pursue ambitious projects, to choose your own direction. "Fate" exits the stage.

Pluto, ruling your career and worldly standing, spends 2009 to 2025 in your "background" zone — of gov't, institutions, administration, management, nursing, warehousing, research, spas and resorts, sympathy and empathy. That makes this area fertile for advancement and status growth. However, in 2019 the Moon's south node also occupied this sector, laying a cloud of delay, temptation, false promise and disappointment over this zone. That cloud remains until May 5, so step lightly in this background sector until then. After May 5, to year's end, this cloud shifts to socializing, groups, light romance, etc. (That's not depressing — read "Love" above.) The significant news is, from May onward you're freed to charge after your ambitions in this background zone once again, with huge good luck!

Office politics and schmoozing raise your profile January to mid-February. Hard, hands-on work, rolling up your sleeves, adds to your success January through April. Your high energy and confidence boost your chances, makes you a leader, in February. However, don't start any new earnings projects — especially a business — mid-February to mid-March. (They would collapse in confusion, or worse, slowly bleed your time, efforts and money while you kept holding on, hoping.)

April's for making contacts, travel, new office or telephone systems. You have the intensity and determination to push through reforms — or merely to reach out and make new career-enhancing contacts.

Play it slow in May — you're a bit sluggish, and would rather be napping at home than preening in head office. June's more for romance than hard work, but it does offer fruitful rewards from simple, hard work. However, keep an eye open for mistakes and supply shortages mid-June to mid-July. Don't begin new projects or ventures. July also rewards hard work, and, after mid-month, is a good time to hire employees (or to seek employment). (Before mid-July, if seeking work, contact former employers, or return to a past kind of work.)

August/September brings opportunities, negotiations, agreements and contracts — and possible competition. Be diplomatic and eager to "merge." Results will please you. In October, research, secrets, and legal/travel/international/media themes work their way into your business or career efforts — but don't start any new ventures mid-October to mid-November, and watch/protect ongoing projects regarding delays, misunderstandings, indecision and false starts. A former career/job role might return. There will be a lot of discussion about your business or career all October and most of November. You might be attracted to your boss, or his/her son or daughter. I don't recommend this one. In late November to mid-December, higher-ups favour you, so make proposals, present your ideas, even ask for a promotion. And have fun — gatherings welcome you, and you will be a hit at company parties, seminars, conventions, etc.

HOME / FAMILY:

Uranus, your ruling planet, and a purveyor of unexpected, sudden events, inventiveness, nerd-i-ness and expanding friendship, spends 2018 to 2026 in your domestic sector. This will bring a "revolution" in your domestic situation. More friends will gather around your fireplace (especially in January/February) as your social life, always strong, now revolves around your residence.

2020 is generally a quiet time for you, with private luck and joys more rewarding than public involvements. This will draw you even more to your home. It's a good year to work on repairs, improvements, even construction of a new home. For young couples, pregnancy becomes a cherished goal. If this becomes elusive, seek medical advice. You might adopt, or, if you marry now, your new spouse might bring step-children.

From 2018 to 2026, your children are/will be bright, social, buoyant in spirit, inventive and a joy to watch. You will focus on them almost to the exclusion of other matters. If there was a vote to name the "Parents of the Decade," you'd be the winner! But in 2020 kids might be a little more nervous or stressed, and youngsters can be impulsive, so watch them carefully around traffic or other dangerous situations. One note: children born 2018-2026 (and kids of any age during this period) will be stubborn — and won't budge an inch if they dig in their heels. To dissolve bad behaviour, use two things: affection, and logic/intelligence. And your secret weapon: tell them that bad behaviour will reduce their number of friends. (For these kids, friends are more important than almost anything else.)

April to June (mildly) and late December into 2021/22 (strongly) will bring important domestic decisions based on practical or (not sure why?) governmental factors.

If you want to move or buy a new home, 2020 is a pretty good time. It helps you find a good retreat, in a neighbourhood that will please you. January, mid-March, May and late August/early September are good house-hunting times.

March brings family harmony. A great time, after the 10th, to beautify your home. Enlist the children, if you have them. They'll enjoy it, and they'll do a very passable job!

In June, the kids will both delight you and puzzle you. September is a good time for a family trip or adventure.

FINANCES / INVESTMENT / DEBT:

Since 2011, and lasting to 2025, your income will generally swell, especially if you let yourself be guided by intuition, hunch, sympathy and caring. You might start giving to charity. (The way karma works, the more charitable you are, the more willing the cosmos will be to direct money your way.) If you're poor, it will be easy to find charity, gov't aid, etc. Disability payments —also easy. If you're seeking employment, look toward warehousing, nursing, civil service and medical professions — better after April.

Investments are similar. From January through April, avoid investing in these same areas (warehouses, hospitals, etc.). But they do offer good returns, good investments, during the remainder of the year. Your wisest investments, January to May 5, will be in tools, machinery, daily health aids (e.g., vitamin companies) personnel agencies, appliance manufacturers…

From April to August, you can profit by taking a bit of a gamble — or by investing in art, vacation resorts, toys, love-related items, luxury goods (not status goods).

May/June bring in more money, but also imbue you with an almost subconscious urge to spend. Fight it — use extra income to pay down debt, rather than waste it on impulsive purchases.

July brings funds from work — but don't invest before mid-month. August holds opportunities — some at a distance — and might reward you for forming an association or partnership of interests. September is your strongest investment — and debt reduction month. August through October favours financial actions. But make no new investments or $ projects mid-October to November 3. After the 3rd, November highlights your career or business efforts, and might give you a chance to ask for a pay raise, or to raise your fees/prices a little. Reject December's financial enticements, should they occur — promises, temptations, might hide subtle difficulties.

HEALTH:

Note: I am not a doctor, so these comments are general, and do not necessarily apply to you.

You often have some trouble with your legs, Aquarius. If you feel weakness in this area, the cause might be a lack of iron, or a nervous condition (e.g., spinal stenosis). In 2020, if you feel any dizziness, leg weakness, or walk "like a sailor" (lurching mildly side-to-side) see a doctor. Your stomach/digestion might be a bit uncertain; if so, nerves can be the cause. Your daily health is good through April. Avoid entering hospital, January to April.

From May 2020 through all 2021 institutions, hospitals, will be very effective in fixing whatever ails you. You'll be very active July to December, so don't strain an ankle or bang a knee as you rush about. This Spring, and again late December into 2021/22, your connections with institutions will grow, and be serious and, potentially, profitable. But these periods might also make your teeth/gums, bones, knees and skin more vulnerable.

PISCES

February 19 – March 20

Start nothing significant or important:
February 16 to March 9
June 18 to July 12
October 13 to November 3.

GENERAL:

This is really your decade, Pisces, from 2011 to 2025. You become yourself, you find your core and your voice. This empowers you to pursue the most significant goals of your life.

Casual friends and contacts will be instrumental in earning money — the larger your circle of contacts, the more money you'll make, from 2018 to 2026. The good thing: your circle of friends will grow, as friendship, kindness and inventiveness flows between you and others. Expect to make some new associations.

Until May, passion, deep romance and creativity bless you, while social pleasures somehow undercut your goals. But from May onward, your social delights and light flirtations will increase two-fold! Also from May onward, domesticity and security offer a smooth, fruitful path, while seeking status or prestige will impede your progress. This is a splendid year to change or improve your home, but NOT your career or employer.

May to December (and beyond) social joys bless you. You can increase your popularity through small, deliberate steps. A friendly romance might begin. If it starts in August/September, it could turn to marriage.

For a couple of years, your wishes and hopes have been rather serious and sober. 2020 continues this trend, but it's staring to break up, like the ice in spring thaw. In fact, this Spring, late March through June, temporarily eliminates these sober, "wet blanket" influences — a harbinger of 2021, when your dreams and goals will move into an area you like: management, policy, gov't, institutions and health/social welfare.

LUCK:

"Luck" is always of two kinds: the normal, daily or monthly luck that Jupiter (optimism and great worldly luck) and Venus (sweet love, attractions, and mild but good luck). And "karma," the ongoing result of actions we took and patterns we started and wove in the past, that now is rewarding us, or wrapping us in the punishing, restricting web of our own actions/consequences.

Jupiter:

This planet rules grand good luck, and for you specifically it rules career and status. In 2020, Jupiter Will occupy your sign of wishes come true, optimism, popularity and group affairs. The result should be obvious: a boost up the ladder of success seems almost certain! (Unless your hopes lie in a completely different area, such as missionary work. Yet even in this, you would find you were respected, looked up to for some reason.) Your career will benefit from schmoozing, seminars, company picnics, conventions, etc. — though unreliably January through April, and magnificently May to December. Read "Karma" below for more details.

Venus:

Venus rules love, affection and mild good luck for everyone. For you, it also rules casual friends and short trips, and secrets, sex and major finances. From April to early August, this sweet planet favours you immensely in domestic and security areas, making it a fine time to purchase a home, or invest in real estate, security systems, gardening and child-related products, whether in your own home, or on the stock market.

Karma:

From January to May 5, your "good karma" lies in passion, art, creativity, self-expression, raising/teaching children, sports/games, beauty, pleasure — and heavy romance. But you will be "karmically stymied" if you try to play the field in love, or avoid deep romance in favour of social activities, or chase popularity. Chasing these can actually sully your reputation.

From May 5 to year's end (and into 2021) "karma" says you will fail if you directly pursue career success, but succeed if you focus on home, children, real estate. (Read these sections for more clues.)

LOVE:

Through April, you will be wise, mellow and "blessed" in heavy romance. (And will find "social romance" or playing the field, is a dry well.) However, the picture turns 180 degrees, May to December — during these eight months, light, flirty, playful love, juggling two or more options/suitors, and broad socializing, all these tap you with a cheerful wand of good fortune. You might meet "the one" at a gathering.

Oddly, at the same time, May to year's end, love becomes more "down home." Your love for the kids, for your family and abode, will swell. If single, you might find budding romance in your neighbourhood (rather than far away). If you do fall in love, or already are that way, you might (wisely, correctly) nudge your love toward domesticity, toward living together.

January lights flirty fires, but you would be better off chasing exciting, thrilling, even heart-pounding/embarrassing romance. Someone who looks like a mate prospect appears in February and mid-March to mid-April…but if he/she first appears from February 16 to March 9, she/he'd better be a former flame, or it will never end in a marriage or long-term amour. In March, a friend could become an intimate partner. (You attract attention easily this month.)

Late April and May might bring love's excitement, but a hidden burden lies under the surface. Your sexual magnetism surges mid-May through June — in June, a viable prospective life-mate appears, and you won't be shy about chasing him/her. But mid-June to mid-July again advises against forming a brand new relationship — instead, keep your eyes open for an old flame.

July is strongly romantic. A co-worker affair might send you into "puzzled pleasure" in August/September. September/October brings peer-to-peer opportunities — you might feel excited and frustrated by an attractive person. (Partly because his/her focus on details drives you a bit crazy.) October is sexy — reject extra-marital temptations. Again, mid-October to early November might bring a former flame.

November's sweet, love is gentle and far-seeing. December's for career, not love — but an intimate memory (or bed mate) lingers early on.

Casual sex is available from July to year's end. The question is: do you sense a long-term relationship with this person, or decades of mild boredom? Look ahead, then decide.

CAREER / BUSINESS:

If you want to change careers, employers, do it well before May. From May 5 2020 to January 2022, do not change careers or switch employers. Your present position/work environment (or business) might seem boring, suffocating, restrictive, without upward prospects — but if you change now, your new position, shining with promise at first, will soon become as stultifying and limited as your present one, with one crucial difference: your present position will "right itself" by 2022, whereas any new position, entered before January 2022, will always be the opposite of satisfying.

So stay where you are, keep your head down and stick with the status quo. Don't push bosses (or VIPs anywhere). If they reject or "file" your brilliant proposal, shrug and accept it. If you present it again, or push in any way, higher-ups will push back, and you won't like that!

In the broadest terms, you would be better off to quit than to switch. In fact, it is possible you will earn more from "retreating" than from staying put, especially April to early August. (You might earn two times your annual salary from one real estate project — see the "Home" section below.)

Another solution: Instead of pushing higher-ups, May onward, turn your energy toward the social sides of your vocation — show affection to co-workers, organize company golf tournaments, volunteer to conduct or attend seminars, ask to be on a convention committee. This way, you'll have fun, your job will not seem so weighty or boring, and you'll make a far better impression on higher-ups. This period is a super one for sales people, lobbyists and professional schmoozers.

Your career planet, Jupiter, sets up beneficial conditions in early January (especially with "head office" or gov't agencies) late April into May (communications, paperwork) July (opportunities but perhaps also opposition, competition) September (wisdom) and late November into December (culmination of a project?).

HOME / FAMILY:

In domestic zones, 2020 will be a year to remember (fondly, not negatively!). From April 4 to August 7, the loving planet Venus sits in your sector of home, family, property and security. If you are planning a big home-related project — renovations, building a home, landscaping, bringing a baby into the world, changing homes, buying/selling real estate — time it for this period. (Best April to mid-May, and July 11 to August. The 57 days in-between might bring a temporary lull or delay — that's okay, just be patient. But it's probably wise not to start domestic projects in these 57 days.)

This entire Spring/Summer brings family affection and harmony. Your children will feel more loved and secure, which in turn makes them more loveable and better behaved. It also helps you find the money for these projects — the bank will give you a mortgage or credit line more easily than most years.

In January, seek co-operation with your spouse. A good time to dream about and discuss the future (but not to initiate firm plans). In February, your spouse follows your lead — which has mixed results, as you grow indecisive mid-month to mid-March. I've already described April to August above.

August is a great month for hands-on work on the home — painting, etc. (September, too, but a bit less so.) Children will display new talents — a good time to enroll them in arts and other courses — from dancing to karate. Be "present" for your spouse in September — it's your most important bond.

October brings sexual temptation, which can arise when you have other couples over. Reject it firmly: such selfish foolery can bring a whole house down. A legal problem from the past might also arise (about a 10 % chance). November can solve this problem or expand it, depending on your reaction. Otherwise, this is a good month for a family trip, for culture, finding good tutors.

Your ambitions are high in December; be willing to forgo domestic concerns for awhile.

FINANCES / INVESTMENT / DEBT:

Money will gush toward you from July through year's end. Good — very good. But at the same time, you'll be spurred by an almost subconscious urge to spend (and contract debt) — stop yourself! With self-discipline, you can end this year with a far fatter bank account than you entered with. But if you can't control spending, you could actually exit 2020 poorer. This "money gush" might slow temporarily from mid-September to mid-November — or money comes from the distant past. (Someone pays an old debt?)

Your investment planet, Venus, helps you pick winners mid-January to early February. Be cautious mid-February through March — you're too impulsively hopeful. (That said, a cautious entry into social zones could pay off. Social = night clubs, dance halls, gathering places, convention and public relations companies, etc.)

Investment in real estate, security companies/systems, furniture, paint manufacturers, makers of any domestic items, from cutlery to diapers, garden and nursery firms, house builders — these favour you from April to early August.

For most of August, anything to do with motherhood might profitably draw your investment dollars. Machinery, appliance and tool manufacturers — or investing directly in machinery (e.g., buying an excavator) — can prove rewarding August and September.

October favours putting your money into travel, international companies, import/export, law firms, cruise lines, cosmetic surgery (e.g., "Clear Choice" dental implants) and education providers. (If you're young, investing in an education should have lifetime rewards.) November's similar (put money in travel, etc.) but might also offer some of the "purest" investments of the whole year. The second half of December advises investing in your career, or in status symbols.

HEALTH:

Note: I am not a doctor, so these comments are general, and do not necessarily apply to you.

Like almost everything about you, Pisces, your health (or illnesses) are elusive and often hard to pin down. Your feet are often bothersome — stock up on Epsom salts or other foot-relaxers. Be careful when running or rushing. From May to December, try to stay out of the hospital. Sun stroke and sunburn are always a threat these last 8 months — but easily avoided. Be careful with cosmetics, sugar overload, and ill-fitting clothes (tight shoes!). This Spring, protect or improve your skin, bones, knees, and teeth/gums. In general, a healthy year!

— **THE END** —

Manufactured by Amazon.ca
Bolton, ON